I Just Haven't Met You Yet

Book Design & Production:
Columbus Publishing Lab
www.ColumbusPublishingLab.com

Paperback ISBN: 978-1-63337-686-1
E-Book ISBN: 978-1-63337-687-8

Printed in the United States of America
1 3 5 7 9 10 8 6 4 2

I Just Haven't Met You Yet

An Open Letter to
Future Generations

Penny Deaton

To my future grandchildren.

I am Penny Deaton. I am a child of God, wife, mother of three, mother-in-law to one, daughter, sister, friend to many, and retired teacher of children with special needs.

My purpose for writing this book is to share my faith—how and why I believe in Jesus Christ—to encourage you to discover your gifts and use them, to reassure you through different seasons of life, and to influence you to learn and to wonder. I hope this book will help children.

How am I going to do this? I will use examples from my life experiences; Bible scriptures will reinforce my messages; scientific research will support my guidance to you; and I will use music and hopefully humor to enhance important points.

At the end of every chapter, I've posed questions to help you share your thoughts, feelings, or beliefs. You can share as much as you feel comfortable sharing. These questions may also provide children with an opportunity to ask their parents or grandparents questions, learning from their experiences and gaining their insight.

This journey of writing a book has been a blessing to my life. I hope reading it will be a blessing to your life as well.

I give thanks to God, my family, and friends.

Thank you for choosing *I Just Haven't Met You Yet*.

Penny

Introduction

My dad lost his two-year battle with pancreatic cancer in December 2018. That winter my mom went on a rampage, cleaning out papers, closets, and drawers—I think it was her way of escaping the void she felt living alone. They had been married fifty-eight years. In this cleaning frenzy, my mom came across a poem written by my dad's mother, published in the 1984 *American Poetry Anthology*.

I am fourteenth in a line of sixteen grandchildren. My grandmother and I never spent much time alone together. I'm not sure why. Maybe I was too young or simply do not remember. Sifting through hazy memories, I remember her on the farm, a little old lady who looked ninety with white hair, farm dress and apron, and silver, horn-rimmed glasses. Even her name was old: Gladys. Gladys and Herman, my step-grandfather. For the twenty-plus years I knew my grandmother, she always looked the same. She was meek and mild-mannered with a sharp mind, soft voice, and gentle laugh.

When I was little, my family spent many Sunday afternoons driving to the country, down the mile-long lane for a visit and Sunday meal with my grandparents. Jeff, my older brother, and I ran around the henhouse, the outhouse, the big old barn, and the small side house where squirrel tails hung. We occasionally picked green apples from the massive overgrown apple tree and hopped over the rotten ones on the ground. We also hopped over the cow patties in the field and swung on the old tire swing in the backyard.

But I can't think of one conversation I had with my grandma. Why didn't I talk to her more? Why didn't she talk to me? Why didn't I ever help her? She was always busy; there was work to be done. Maybe she just wasn't one of those grandmas who doted on her grandchildren. (My other grandma was the doting grandma. Sadly, we lost her when I was very young. In case you're wondering, I would definitely be the doting grandma.) I'm sure Grandma loved us. She loved us so much she let us city kids run around on the farm instead of making us help out. As I read her poem, I came to realize that I did not know my grandmother very well. I thought, *Who is this person? That is not the grandma I remember!* I was pleasantly surprised, and I regretted not knowing her better.

I don't have any grandchildren yet, and by the time I do, I most likely won't have much opportunity to get to know them very well either. For many families of the 1950s and '60s, including mine, women graduated from high school, married their high school sweetheart, got pregnant, lived in the same small town as their family, and raised a family with the help and support of relatives. That's what my mom did. She was a stay-at-home mom who did the majority of the child-rearing on her own while my dad went to work to provide for us. Relatives were always part of our lives; most were close enough to visit frequently.

I graduated from high school in the '80s, went to college, got married, and settled into my teaching career for several years. Then I got pregnant. We went on to raise our family with the aid of grandparents young enough and close enough to help. My children have now graduated from high school, gone to college, and are settling into their careers. One is married. The other two are unattached. Now they travel around the world, enjoy each other's company, and reach for goals in their careers; they want to be more financially stable before settling down and starting a family.

I figure by the time any one of them has children old enough for me to be an influence in their lives, I will be in my late sixties or early seventies. And I will only see them a few times a year since they will not live near me. As a woman, by the age of sixty-five I have a one-in-five chance of having Alzheimer's (Alzheimers.net). This statistic is staggering to me! Remembering new names has always been a struggle for me, and remembering names I already know is increasingly difficult. I have trouble retrieving a particular word I need, constantly forget where I parked at the grocery store, and have an inability to recall recent conversations—all signs that make me wonder if I will be that one out of five. Those odds are scary. Not only will I be older when I have grandchildren, they may view me as the grandma in Ohio who doesn't even remember them.

This is one of the reasons I have been prompted to write a book to my future grandchildren. In case my mind is weak when we meet, I want you to know who I am and what I believe. There have been other people in my life who struggle with their beliefs. So I hope—no, I pray—that this book will give you some guidance or at least something to ponder. I am writing this book for you, my grandchildren.

On a side note, if you're someone reading this book who needs some advice from a grandma, it's for you too. It would be my pleasure to take on some additional grandchildren and provide you with extra guidance, support, and love from another grandma—even if it's just for the duration of you reading this book. Who doesn't want an extra grandma? When I say grandchildren, I'm talking to you too. I think it is highly likely that the things I tell you and what I worry about are very similar to what your grandma would like to say to you too, if she hasn't already.

You have great parents, so I don't doubt that you are loved, nurtured, and cared for. However, I don't want my grandchildren to grow up in a world with so many other worldly influences without having my say too. If we don't talk to our children and grandchildren, believe me when I say: The world most certainly will.

I have lived long enough to learn a thing or two. Experience is the best teacher. This book shares some of the lessons I've learned along the way. My beliefs and ideas are not necessarily new, although some of the crazy ones are all mine. I want to share select experiences and sermons that have stood out to me, so you don't have to learn every lesson on your own the hard way.

I will let you in on a little secret that no one ever told me: The decisions you are making now are important. I always thought that I would make all the big decisions when I became an adult. Being an adult does come with some big decisions. However, looking back, I've come to believe that the decisions you make now and in the next five or six years will have a dramatic impact on the direction your life will go. The decisions you make right now *matter*. I want to help you make choices that will make your journey a little easier, and also to be sure you are exposed to Christianity.

Does this mean that if you read this book and follow my advice you won't have any problems? No, it does not. You're going to lead your own life and have your own joys and struggles. Does it mean that the decisions you'll be making soon will put you on a path leading directly where you want to go? Probably not. People make changes at all stages of life. I don't know anyone who started off in the perfect life right off the bat and then continued to have a perfect life with no changes or challenges. Life evolves as you live it. You'll meet people, have experiences, and learn about yourself as you go. You'll have to work hard to attain certain aspects. Change is inevitable. That's what makes life so great. It is unpredictable.

However, I do believe that you will make very important choices in the next few years. Again, the decisions you make now *matter*. They will help you find your footing as an adult. I want to help you make decisions that will lead you to be happy and successful and (I pray to God) Christian.

It's not that I've lived a tough life, so I have so many lessons to share. Quite the opposite. Well, I've not led a super privileged life by any means, but I've had a blessed life with a couple road bumps on the journey. These are a few of the insights I've gained along the way.

I am a Christian, and as a Christian, the single most important thing for me to share with you is my belief in and love for God. It saddens me to think you might grow up not knowing Him. I'm not sure what you will be taught about religion. Since this topic is of utmost importance to me, I'm going to assume maybe you don't know God or believe in Him. I will try to persuade you to think otherwise by sharing my thoughts and how He has worked in my life.

Once you have become a Christian and experienced God's love, you want to share it with everyone. But when Christians become too outspoken, it turns people off. People tend to tune out. So, I usually go about my day being kind to others, smiling, hoping I emit God's love in some subliminal way. I question the effectiveness of either approach. My quandary becomes: Do I quote a bunch of scripture to you from a book and a God you may or may not believe in, or do I write a bunch of flowery uplifting stuff and keep my fingers crossed that you'll see God's light in me? I love you too much to leave it to chance. Offering encouragement and speaking kindly is a wonderful way to be, but that still leaves too much ambiguity to my purpose for you. I try not to be too overbearing with the God talk, but it is so much a part of who I am that it's difficult for me to give you advice without mentioning God. He's had such a powerful influence in my life, and He will in the lives of all who know Him. My balance will lie in-between, when you see how I am just an average person with plenty of faults trying to live a Godly life. I try to "keep it real" because I am far from perfect, yet God is still always there for me. You need to know He is available to you too.

Therefore, I ask you to consider the possibility that God is real and wants to be a part of your life (if He isn't already). My goal is for you to discover and experience the joy that Christians have. When you follow God, you will be blessed, and your life will be richer in ways you cannot imagine. It's the best gift I can pass down to you, and I want you to know that I have prayed for you many, many times. I just haven't met you yet.

This is my grandma's poem:

It's Never Too Late

It's never too late, my friend, to say
You're sorry for words and deeds
That may have been said and done
Without thinking, to your fellow man.
Go out of your way to do something nice
For someone, who needs a little more than advice.
It's knowing and doing the things that we should
Not knowing and hoping that other folks would.
It's never too late to show you care
For family and neighbors and friends.
Yes, go out of your way and you'll never regret it
For every good deed returns more than expected.
Go out of your way to help those in need
Of attention and friendship. Don't falter or waiver
Your life will be blest when you take that first step
And you'll reap the reward, if you do someone a favor.
It's never too late to ask God for help
To guide and direct you in all that you do,
Your life will be changed and richer, by far,
For it isn't too late for me nor for you.
—Gladys Offenbacher

CHAPTER 1

Earth

Before I share my life's lessons with you, I want to tell you why I am a Christian. This is the foundation of who I am, and God's love will be a consistent thread throughout these lessons. I have prayed that you will be introduced to God and Christianity, and I hope both are already important parts of your life. If not, you will have to bear with me throughout this book. Please keep an open mind. If nothing else, you will come to know me and my beliefs.

I am not a scientist. This will be painstakingly obvious to many. I earned the minimal science credits needed to graduate with a bachelor's degree and a master's in education. Science wasn't even my favorite subject in school. Although be aware: your interests will change and expand throughout life.

Whenever I see signs that read, *I believe in science*, I assume that means, *I don't believe in God*. For me, science is one of the very reasons I *do* believe in God. It's so difficult for me to grasp the idea that our beautiful, magnificent, sophisticated (I struggle to find words sufficient to describe it) home, Earth, came to exist accidentally.

If you don't believe that Earth was created by God, I assume you believe it was formed according to some other theory: the Big Bang, an electrical spark, gravity collapsing causing dust and gas to spin, or some other random occurrence. Those are your two choices: God or chance.

I want to pause here and give a brief vocabulary lesson. *Random* is defined as "proceeding, made, or occurring without definite aim, reason, or pattern." (dictionary.com)

Does Earth have aim or purpose? Life.

Is the Earth reasonable in its structure? Various formations of land, plants, air, water, etc. to support life.

Does Earth have a pattern? Seasons/days/years/etc. Time.

Nothing about our home is random.

Imagine that a huge collision in space not only created this Earth, but that Earth just so happened to operate in a consistent and timely way. It would be quite astonishing that randomness *formed* the Earth, *placed* it perfectly, and made it *function* with precision. I need to address each of these treasures.

First of these three treasures, the odds that Earth came into existence randomly are one in 700 quintillion, according to discovermagazine.com. After that mind-boggling statistic, the teacher and visual learner in me wants to clarify exactly what a seven with twenty zeros looks like: 1 in 700,000,000,000,000,000,000.

According to Sir Fred Hoyle, an astronomer, those odds are roughly comparable to rolling double-sixes 50,000 times in a row with unloaded dice (icr.org). I compare it to going to Vegas and saying, "I'll put my soul for eternity on red," on a wheel with one red and 699... quintillion blacks. That's a risky bet.

Science and math are cousins, right? Quora states that "science generally uses mathematics as a tool to describe science. Science is a body of knowledge about the Universe. Mathematics is a language that can be used to describe relationships and change in relationships in a rational way (quora.com). Either way, science or math, I trust both. I am a firm believer in looking at the numbers to make decisions in my life. One thing we can all agree on is that statistics are very helpful. We all use math every day. As an educator, I measured the progress, individual goals, and daily performance of each student; quarterly performances and much more. It drove my instruction. This was etched into my professional brain. As a teacher, you must be a numbers person to some extent.

When our son almost died after his first surgery for a congenital heart defect (I'll discuss this in Chapter 10), we heard about a surgeon in Michigan with a 90-percent-plus success rate specializing in his heart defect. We high-tailed it to Michigan. It was a no-brainer! I have lived by numbers from the everyday stuff to the big stuff.

Secondly, after the miraculous formation of Earth, I am awed by its placement in the solar system. Science says that if *any* aspects of Earth's placement were off even a little bit, it would disrupt Earth's ability to sustain life (glob.adw.org).

The distance from the sun prevents water from boiling or freezing; water is distributed evenly in a cycle.

The Earth's orbit around the sun allows the temperature to remain relatively constant.

The sun puts out a steady amount of energy.

The tilt of Earth's axis creates our experience of seasons without making them too extreme.

Other factors that make this a habitable zone in the galaxy are Earth's molten core and magnetic fields that protect us from the most harmful rays of the sun, the rapid rotation of the Earth, the moon providing tidal zones that do not destroy life, and nearby gas giants that attract asteroids and comets, which keeps them from hitting Earth.

It's all placed perfectly. There is not an improvement that needs to be made. The science of it all is amazing.

Third, the way Earth functions in a timely manner is equally impressive. Now, I realize that every planet has a timeline as well, but ours also coincides quite nicely with life and what our bodies need to function. For one thing, is it just a coincidence that doctors suggest seven to eight hours of sleep every night, when Earth provides just that in darkness? I also understand that some believe that because Earth won that "existence lottery," this is why we have life. I just find it too coincidental that they complement each other so well.

This concept of time is a big component in my proof of God's design. Earth's position in space, tilt toward the sun, spin on its axis, and revolution around the sun, all undeviating in their duration of seconds, minutes, hours, days, etc., combine to form our days and nights and seasons: winter, spring, summer, to fall. These all happen consistently year after year, down to the second, every day. Again, nothing about our home is random.

Have you ever noticed the signs at the beach that announce the high and low tide *to the minute*? That alone impresses me! We *always* know when high and low tide will be. These are printed in the *Farmer's Almanac* before the year begins. That means you can pick a day, any day in the future, and know what time the tide will come in or out. It is difficult to understand how a randomly made object could perform with such precision and predictability. Randomness does not operate that way.

Another vocabulary review: A *scientific law* is "based on repeated experimental observations that describe some aspect of the world" (definitions. net). There are many, many scientific laws because of the repeated experiments and observations that were proven to be true in our natural world *consistently*. I understand that many of these laws are laws because of the way Earth was formed. However, I do not believe that an Earth made randomly would operate under a whole host of laws that are consistent. Randomness does not generate consistency, especially in such a multitude of ways.

When scientists study a particular subject, they take out all of the randomness they can, controlling all of the factors they can to prove their hypothesis. Everything about science is based on precision. So I find it difficult to believe that everything in this world is exact and explicit except its conception.

I submit the beauty on this Earth as proof of God, but I suppose an unbeliever would see this as spontaneous formations over billions of years.

I see the beauty of a sunset and sunrise, the forests, deserts, oceans, valleys, mountains, and all the gorgeous sites from every season that He created for us. His artistry is so amazing! Words and explanations cannot compete with the beauty we have been provided. God has given us intelligence to build skyscrapers, perform surgeries, fly around the world, use computers and telephones, have electricity, and can we not forget indoor plumbing! I wonder what we will come up with next given His resources to us. Science does explain our ever-changing environment, but it does not account for the "awe" effect. One cannot measure elegance and the feelings it stirs. As much as I respect and believe in science, it doesn't compare to the overall exquisiteness I *feel* blessed with. When I see the beauty in this world, all of the scientific logic becomes an insignificant blur in my mind. I become in awe of the supreme power of His design.

Not only has God created this massive sphere, He also created everything right down to the parts we can't see with the naked eye. Have you ever thought about the invisible life that exists in the air around us? I don't mean the gases that make up the air, but also the radiation, ultraviolet/light/sound waves, gamma rays, bacteria, fungi, viruses, germs, mites, and creatures that live on your face and body. This host of invisible life can be very disturbing if you think about it too much. I believe that we would be shocked if we could see what is going on right in front of our faces. It all works masterfully, from the unseen germs, waves, etc., to the vast, unseen universe. I believe all creation has a purpose and a plan from a skillful architect.

Isn't the complexity of it all fascinating? But here's the lie that the world wants you to believe: you have to choose between science and God. They believe that only a randomly made world could have many scientific layers to it. I guess they believe that Christians think an all-knowing, omnipotent God would *not* create a world that is scientific and logical? It's more of a stretch to believe that randomness created science than for God to have created science.

I want you to know that Christians believe in science, although the two do not completely mesh in all ways. There are some unexplainable issues, but I believe the two do not always coincide because God does not want them to. None of us have all the answers, because *He does not want it to be*. God does not want to provide us with obvious answers. In this way, He generates faith within us to bridge those gaps, and he inspires us to keep seeking Him in the questions this world generates. If God pre-loaded us with all the answers, we might as well be little robots with no curiosity for this magnificent world, and no effort or sincerity behind our love for Him. Love is not real love when it's forced. God has given us the choice to love Him and believe in Him or not. Part of making the right choice is accepting that there will be things that will be beyond our understanding.

I accept that my brain as a mere mortal will never be able to understand what He can do and how everything works. The Creator of this place is supreme. But this doesn't stop me from wondering, based on what I've learned from science and what has been told to me in the Bible. I'm all for studying, questioning, and learning everything we can. We were designed to think! But I'm okay knowing that I will never know everything. That's called faith. God wants us to believe and choose Him without providing us with a blueprint on life and how He orchestrated everything.

My husband and I recently went to hear a friend of ours preach. His name is Eric Barto, author of *HOPE: Having Ongoing Purpose for Eternity*. Eric was diagnosed with brain cancer in 2004 and given one year to live. At the time of this publishing, it's 2022. Eric has been living for the Lord since his cancer diagnosis. One thing that stood out to me as he preached was his insight into faith. "If you believe, you will receive whatever you ask for in prayer." (Matthew 21:22) (There is more information about prayer in Chapter 10.) Believe, *then* you will receive. You must choose God first before you can receive His gifts. Just like any love worth having, it has to be a choice, because if He programmed us to love Him or provided us with solid data of His existence, we wouldn't have to choose Him.

If you're looking for hard proof that there is a God, there is none. You have to make the choice: God or randomness. Be brave enough to have faith and choose God, and He *will* come alive in your life. God's message to us is this: "For we live by faith, not by sight." (2 Corinthians 5:7)

You have a 1 in 700,000,000,000,000,000,000 chance that I am wrong, that there is no God, and that randomness defines us and our world. Is that a wager you're willing to make when your life and the eternity of your soul are at stake? *I believe this is the most important decision you'll ever make in your life.* Only *you* can make it. Believe me, if I could do it for you, I would. And out of love for you, I'd choose the Creator.

• • • CHAPTER 1 QUESTIONS • • •

1. Have you ever had to choose between science and God?
2. Defend a decision you made based on numbers/facts/statistics.

SCIENCE SAYS THAT WE NEED AT LEAST FOUR BASIC ELEMENTS TO SURVIVE.

1. Water
2. Air
3. Food
4. Light

AND LOOK WHAT THE BIBLE TELLS US ABOUT JESUS

1. I am the Living Water
2. I am the Breath of Life
3. I am the Bread of Life
4. I am the Light of the World

SCIENCE WAS RIGHT, WE NEED JESUS TO LIVE.

He is the Maker of Heaven and Earth, the sea, and everything in them-He remains faithful forever.

PSALM 146:6 NIV

By Him all things were created, in Heaven and on Earth, visible and invisible, whether thrones or dominions or rulers or authorities-all things were created through Him and for Him.

COLOSSIANS 1:16 ESV

CHAPTER 2

The Human Body

Along with the formation, placement, and performance of our Earth, I am equally amazed at the human body. Once again, you would think you have to choose. Do you believe in the Theory of Evolution? Or do you believe in God? I believe in science. Things change. I get it. As a Christian, I also believe the Bible. When God says he created humans on day six, I believe Him. If I have to choose between God's Word and man, I'm going to have faith and believe God's Word. I appreciate how science explores the complexities of His creations, and I cannot ignore science's findings.

Biologos.org says we don't have to choose. It states, "...we see God as crafting and governing the entire evolutionary process to bring about the abundance of species we see today. Of course, it is possible that God supernaturally created each of the species separately, but did so in the pattern that so strongly suggests common ancestry. But doesn't the natural order faithfully testify to its Creator?" It's a lot to ponder. The thought of these processes happening all by themselves, with nothing more than an abundance of passing time, is confusing to me. It is difficult for me to combine my creation beliefs with fossils, genetic codes, etc., but apparently it is possible. God always tells us to trust in His ways even though we want our answers now. I choose God, but it's comforting to know that you can choose both.

Again, I will not be solving this lifelong quandary for mankind. All I can do is share with you what I believe based on a simple look at a human body.

OUR AMAZING, BEAUTIFUL BODIES

The human body is made of major organ systems that work together:

1. Circulatory
2. Respiratory
3. Digestive
4. Excretory
5. Nervous
6. Endocrine
7. Immune
8. Skeletal
9. Muscular
10. Reproductive
11. Integumentary

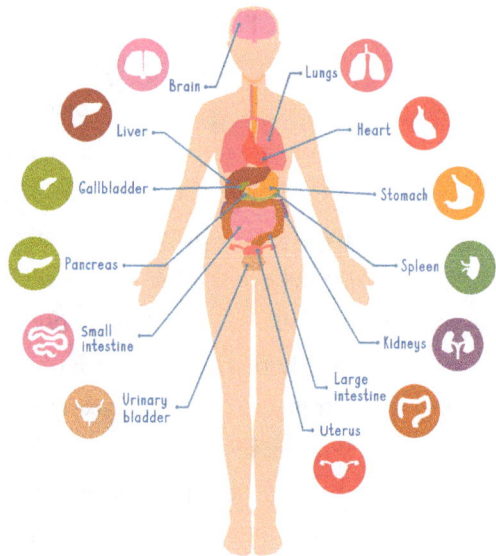

Just look at each one of these systems! Look at it and allow yourself to be awed by the complexity of so many bodily components working together in harmony! When I think of these systems working together in a human, I am simply amazed. The reproduction process alone overwhelms me!

Did you ever think about how everything we put into our bodies is also beautiful? Food is beautiful! I enjoy the presentation of a meal at a restaurant. I enjoy eating the common meal from my kitchen. I *really* enjoy a meal from my mom's kitchen. God provided us with such a variety of food that looks so colorful, smells so savory, tastes delicious, has many textures, and—let's not leave out our sense of hearing—sure, they can even entice us with the snap of a carrot stick or pop of popcorn. Years ago, I was introduced to the idea that the foods we eat resemble the body part or organ that the food strengthens. I thought, *How brilliant!* It's so simple! I imagine that unbelievers would call this merely coincidences. I think it's genius.

Picture in your minds each of these foods and realize that the body part they are strengthening looks very similar to it:

a sliced carrot - the human eye

a sliced tomato - has multiple chambers, like the heart

a slice of onion - body cells

a slice of mushroom - ear

red wine - blood

walnut - brain

kidney bean - kidneys

celery stalk - bones

sweet potato - pancreas

grapes - alveoli of the lungs

avocados - uterus

clams - testicles

banana - smile (It contains serotonin, which is happy chemicals, to the brain.)

There are many others. Isn't God's design full of astonishing miracles?

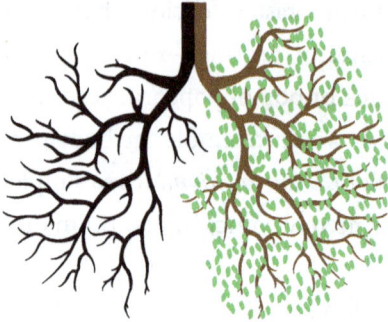

Here is another example I found that is equally awe-inspiring as to the design of God's creation.

"We breathe in what the trees breathe out, and they breathe in what we breathe out. Forever overwhelmed by the beauty of God's design."

By Sabrina Barich

Our Amazing (Not So Beautiful) Bodies

I am sometimes befuddled by God's design. Have you ever wondered why the food that is so good for us—such as beans, broccoli, and garlic—either gives you bad breath or the toots? I think it is rather comical that the stuff exiting our bodies is far from beautiful. The two clash. Frankly, our bodies are quite disgusting as well as exquisite. Boogers, poop, pee, ear wax, toots (I could go on)—it's truly difficult to think of one good thing that exits our bodies. It's as if God said, "I'm going to create these impressive human forms, but watch what's going to come out of them!" (Wink and a nudge.) God certainly does have a sense of humor. Or perhaps, since God despises pride in men so much, I wonder if He built in assurances to keep us at least a little humble.

I debated whether to mention all this to you because, although it is hilarious, it's also a little repugnant. Then, one day it hit me out of the blue: There *is* one thing that does come out of our body that doesn't make you say "Ewwww!" And that is...get ready for it...tears! Of course, right away I searched for Bible verses about tears. Most of them are about weeping, sorrow, the usual sad stuff. But I did come across one verse that stood out to me, Psalm 56:8: "You keep track of all my sorrows. You have collected all my tears in your bottle. You have recorded each one in your book."

There is a history of tear bottles going back to Roman times, the Victorian period of the nineteenth century, and even the American Civil

War. There are tear bottles created even today. Tear bottles have been used for a long time as a sign of respect, position, or love. I'm not sure if it's literal, but God must keep our tears at least figuratively, to bear our pains and sorrows. In the movie *The Shack,* the Holy Spirit collects the man's tears in a little bottle that is (spoiler alert) used to create something beautiful in the end. God helps us through our hardest times if we let Him. He'll use our sorrow to make something beautiful *if* we are living with the Spirit.

I think of all the ways that we shed tears, such as, obviously, sadness. We cry when we are hurting emotionally or physically, or when we're stressed. And the molecular structure of our tears varies based on their purpose. How amazing is that? Cortisol is a stress hormone that is concentrated in tears. You can literally cry out your stress. So have a good cry when you need to. But don't forget, we also cry when we're happy. Have you ever laughed so hard you cried? Those days are the best! Try to keep those as a happy memory to pull out on a day you need a good laugh.

I'm not sure why God designed an astonishing human machine to produce such vile substances, but tears are definitely an important part of our life journey. And our tears can be as unique as snowflakes (sciencealert.com). God is amazing!

I also want to mention that, when God sees us, He doesn't see our physical bodies. These bodies are temporary for our lives here on Earth. In Heaven, we will shed these bodies like pods or a shell. God looks at you and sees your beautiful soul that He created, that lives inside you along with His Spirit. I remind myself of that sometimes when I'm having a bad season, a bad hair day, feeling frumpy, ugly, ill, or many other worldly ills that we can experience. Don't be too hard on yourself as far as your physical appearance goes. We'll talk more about that later. You are a beautiful soul with a purpose, regardless of your physical appearance. "For the Lord sees not as man sees; man looks on the outward appearance, but the Lord looks on the heart." (1 Samuel 16:7)

"Live as if you were to die tomorrow.
Learn as if you were to live forever."
—Mahatma Gandhi

As a teacher, I sometimes thought of the human brain like a road map. When we are born, I believe the map is almost blank, except for a few major roads that come standard with every brain. Then, every experience you have builds a new road, connects a previous road, or adds pavement or a new lane, expanding on previously learned information. Every little thing you do, hear, see, or learn constructs new pathways in your brain.

An article, "Want to Raise Smart, Kind Kids? Science Says Do This Every Day" says that you can literally grow your child's brain when you read to them. The more you read to your child, the more their neurons will grow and connect together (happyyouhappyfamily.com). So read!

This is why you have to learn everything you can! For example: The longest cells in the human body are the motor neurons, which can be up to 4.5 feet long. You don't think you'll ever need to know that Leif Erikson was the first explorer to reach North America? You may think, "Why do I need to know that the Great Wall of China is the only man-made structure visible from space (4,160 miles long)? I'll never use it again in my life!" Well, I disagree. Learning builds paths and connectors in your brain. The more roads you have, the quicker and easier it is to get somewhere—to access information or create new ideas. Do you see how making these connections teaches you how to think? So, do your homework! All of it! It all matters. Learn everything you can. It'll make your life easier in a multitude of ways.

Some people end up with four-lane paved super highways, and some with decent two-lane roads, easy enough to maneuver where they need to go. And yet some of us end up with a gravel or dirt road with lots of potholes, and you're probably thinking there may be some who are still trying to forge a path thorugh an overgrown terrain! Please remember as you travel through life to be kind to all of the different people you meet with all their various kinds of roads. Be kind to everyone. We need to be patient and tolerant of others just like God is patient and tolerant of us. If intelligence is one of the gifts God gave you, then more will be expected from you. The more gifts God has entrusted you with, the more He'll expect you to implement them in your life. We'll discuss your gifts more later.

If I do develop Alzheimer's disease, all of my recently built roads will be demolished, or at the very least stricken with potholes. My short-term memory will eventually be gone. Even some of my major thoroughfares will be full of potholes—possibly shut down permanently, maybe allowing some traffic through on a good day. As we age, it gets harder for brains to make those connections. Scientists have discovered that it is very important to constantly learn new things to make new connections to keep the brain active throughout your lifetime. Other ways to avoid Alzheimer's are proper diet, exercise, meditation, sunshine, a good night's sleep, and socialization (activebeat.com).

While writing this book, I have come to realize that I think a lot through analogies and metaphors. Maybe it's that teacher in me trying to explain, or the visual learner in me trying to make sense of things for myself. Jesus was a teacher who used parables to teach, so I hope he's okay with me making comparisons. Anyway, another analogy follows.

Your Body is a Machine

You've heard this before in health class, I'm sure. This body that you've been blessed with is a machine. This machine requires fuel, which is food; it uses what fuel it needs to perform and disposes of the rest. And the kind of fuel you put into your body matters too. I worry about the crap they put in our food, about eating too much processed food or eating out too much. Obesity is prevalent in 20.6 percent of children twelve to nineteen years old (www.cdc.gov).

Sleep is also important for your body to perform at its maximum capacity. In a 2014 survey, the National Sleep Foundation found that 45% of adults lack adequate sleep, according to Sam Kemmis in The Science of Sleep and Productivity. So I worry about future generations getting enough exercise because so many jobs and entertainments (such as gaming) now require sitting. Our bodies are designed to work. You gotta move. My dad always liked to sweat. He thought it released toxins from your body. It does. There are many other benefits too.

To have a healthy lifestyle, you need to eat properly, exercise, and sleep. This all sounds like a "duh" moment, I know. But you must take care of the body you are given. Life is a gift from God. You have one body, one soul. Science says you triumphed over at least 100 million other sperm to become you (webmd.com). I don't know if you like your body or not, but this is the body you were given here on Earth, so you need to take care of it. Eat balanced meals, sleep eight hours each night, and exercise regularly. "Do you not know that your bodies are temples of the Holy Spirit, who is in you, whom you have received from God? You are not your own; you were bought at a price. Therefore honor God with your bodies." (Corinthians 6:19-20)

People Are Like Cut-out Sugar Cookies

My final thought on the human body is that I think of all humans as—you guessed it—cut-out sugar cookies. We all have the same basic ingredients (all those systems), but we have different sizes, shapes, and colors. We become unique when God adds a dash of talents and gifts and a pinch of vices to each cookie. I guess those could be the sprinkles on top. We'll discuss those later too.

The anatomy of the human body fascinates me. I am impressed not only by the systems and organs but the uniqueness of handwriting, a fingerprint, and the DNA retrieved from a swab in your mouth. We're all the same yet unique—an oxymoron, I know. As my dad used to jokingly say, "It's just like it, only different." I am amazed at how our bodies are reproduced with such uniformity, yet we are each so unique and exquisitely made. "Indeed, the very hairs of your head are all numbered..." (Luke 12:7) and "Before I formed you in the womb I knew you, before you were born I set you apart..." (Jeremiah 14:5) When I consider how we are all made the same, in His image, yet how he loves each one of us uniquely, my mind is baffled once again. Pair this with the toil of intertwining of the science explaining our creation, and it all just comes down to making a choice.

Life is full of choices, decisions you must make. God is waiting for you to choose Him before He will participate in your life. First you believe, *then* you receive his gifts. This is why people who aren't Christians don't get it. They haven't experienced God's presence because they haven't chosen Him. God will leave you alone if that is your choice, even though that is not what He wants.

I believe God created you, me—all of us. He created us, and He loves us. He gives us freedom of choice to love Him. He could've made us all little robots instilled with the proof that he is God. As little automated beings, we would walk around worshipping Him the way He pre-programmed us to. Instead, God gave us free choice. You get to make that choice, and no one can stop you.

In conclusion of these chapters on Earth and humans, both are so impeccably designed. When I close my eyes and think of us living on a rare blue rock in the infinite black sea of space, where we have found nothing that even comes close to our exquisite home, I am mesmerized. We are creations that have been provided with everything we need to survive. How can both masterpieces be incidental when they complement each other so well? How can such sophisticated bodies and their intricate processes be unplanned and spontaneous? I don't mind studying them, exploring, asking questions, wondering, testing, or proving. The fact that we can follow these processes (again, because of their consistency) is proof to me it's all designed. Study away! We are formed to think. Some are trying to figure out how it all works, thinking the grand prize, the final destination, will be proof of exactly how Earth and humans came to be. We're searching for this proof and following scientific steps to attempt to explain masterpieces when we were created with brains that do not have the capacity of all knowing. I struggle to believe that our Earth and our sophisticated bodies were formed through random processes over time. Earth and life. Each is a lavish gem. Each is a masterpiece in its own right.

• • • CHAPTER 2 QUESTIONS • • •

1. Do you think humans evolved or were created?

2. Do you know someone with Alzheimer's?

3. Is there an area where you could treat your body better? How? What do you do that promotes a healthy lifestyle?

4. What is one of your favorite memories? Or have you ever laughed so hard you cried?

5. What are some other benefits to sweating?

We are God's masterpiece. He has created us
anew in Christ Jesus, so we can do good things
He planned for us long ago.

EPHESIANS 2:10 NLT

CHAPTER 3

Snippet in Time

Whenever I think about my most embarrassing moments, the times I've been hurt, or the parts of life that made me sad, they are actually small snippets of time in the whole scheme of my life. This is important for you to understand. When you go through a hard time, it feels like it will never end. But it does. You will look back, and it will be a small snippet of time in your long, wonderful life.

Many people struggle with mental illness or dependency and end up taking it out on their physical body through cutting, overeating or undereating, burning, addiction to alcohol, tobacco, sex, drugs, and especially suicide.

Suicide is the second leading cause of death for fifteen- to twenty-four-year-olds (www.aacap.org). This is another reason I'm writing to you. I fear that you may get so depressed that you'll want to end your life. You'll go through different seasons of life constantly. Suicidal thoughts go beyond a difficult season. I need you to know that whatever bad time you're going through, it's only temporary. It **will** pass and get better. I promise! But I need to distinguish between a bad season and suicidal thoughts.

A Bad Season

You will experience difficult seasons throughout your life. Yes, we all go through crappy days or phases. Some of us get more crap than others, or more crap days than others, and that's not fair. Life is not always fair. But those times are temporary. You'll look back someday and remember and reflect on how this terrible season shaped you. It may have an impact on who you become. It may even be part of forming your purpose.

Or, guess what? If you don't want to look back and remember, you don't have to. It will become a distant memory as you proceed through life. Your life will be filled with thoughts of your schooling, friends, hobbies, career, your spouse, friends, and family. The difficult times in middle and high school become almost non-existent. I hate to tell you this, but even the really good times become hard to remember. As you go through life, your focus changes so many times. I rarely think about anything pertaining to any of my school years on a regular basis, nor have I for many years.

You may not understand the reason for the difficult season you're going through now. I just want you to remember these three things:

Remind yourself:
This will pass.
I'm just in a bad season.
Everyone has bad seasons.

There are times when I've been hurting so bad that I couldn't even pray. I would just say, "Help me, God." He knows my needs. It doesn't have to be a long, wordy prayer explaining what you need. He knows you, and He's just waiting to hear from you. God loves you no matter what. He made you, so there's nothing you can tell Him that He doesn't already know. You don't have to be perfect. He accepts all of us as we are. I feel loved with all of my imperfections.

Even though I've been hurt before, I don't have any experience in those feelings of wanting to leave my life now. When I look back at parts of my life, I still shudder. I can drum up some pretty embarrassing moments. We all have them. Then I tuck them away, way back there, not to be thought of again for a long time. I don't dwell on negative thoughts. Focus on the present and the future.

I've actually come to a place where I've embraced all of the embarrassing and even painful seasons I've gone through. As a Christian, I only have to experience these feelings here on Earth, and I can look forward to a perfect eternity in Heaven. It'll be ideal there. This life is a small snippet compared to eternity; your circumstances now are a small snippet compared to you entire life. When I feel the lows here and now, it helps me appreciate all the glorious highs we also have here. "Not only so, but we also glory in our sufferings, because we know that suffering produces perseverance; perseverance, character; and character, hope." (Romans 5:3-4)

If you're in a difficult season in your relationship to other kids, this is what I suggest:

First of all, get off of social media or whatever is causing your negative thoughts. I realize at school it's impossible to completely disengage. If your problem is there, I bet a teacher may have a way to help you. You can definitely take a step back from your social life outside of school.

Secondly, I suggest that you stay busy in your free time. Keep your mind occupied with something else. When you have too much time with negative thoughts, your mind can go down a dark path. Believe me, I do understand.

Whenever I'm feeling unsure of myself, I have a Bible verse I repeat: "I can do all things through Him who gives me strength." (Philippians 4:13) Find a verse you like and repeat it.

Do anything to keep your mind busy. To fill the void from your social media, here are a few suggestions:

- Read
- Begin a new hobby or practice, or perfect a current one
- Learn to play an instrument or pick up a new sport

- Adopt a fur friend from the shelter
- Volunteer
- Exercise
- That thing in the back of your mind you'd like to try some day: do that
- Read the Bible. "Keep this Book of the Law always on your lips; meditate on it day and night, so that you may be careful to do everything written in it. Then you will be prosperous and successful" (Joshua 1:8).
- Join a youth group (Side note: Church kids, be nice to new people. Include them. Warning church kids and adults can be cliquey just like at school. We church people are not perfect. Sometimes we get too comfortable in our church family. I hope you find a great group. When you find a church you like, you'll have that feeling of belonging.)

If these seem like too much to take on right now, then take smaller steps. Do *something*. Take a shower, hang up some of those clothes piled in your room, take out the trash. While doing so, keep repeating that Bible verse. When bad thoughts creep in, tell the devil to go away, and say the verse again. Redirecting your mind and staying busy with even little things will help you. Then, on a better day, look at the list again and try again.

You're going to forget about the people you're going to school with now, unless you choose to remember them. If you've struggled in school, you get to start over if you go to college. If you have bad experiences in college, start over when you move into the work force. If you have a terrible work place, get another job and try again. You'll eventually find your place. Trust me: It will get better. You'll look back some day and laugh or shudder, but it will just be a distant memory.

I am going to be honest with you though. I still have seasons in life where things don't go as I would like. There will always be bad seasons or phases. Life is not perfect. It is messy. I'm usually very happy, but then there's times when I think, "Could anything else go wrong?" Or, "How could I have been so stupid?" Or, "What is this world coming to?" I realize that's nothing compared to suicidal thoughts, but I want you to understand that life is this constant cycle of good and bad seasons you must go through. If you're in a bad season now, a good season is waiting in the wings if you stick with it.

SUICIDAL THOUGHTS

God gave you the gift of life with a purpose. You are special! This may sound a little harsh, but it's not up to you to end your life sooner than God intends. "'For I know the plans I have for you,' declares the LORD, 'plans to prosper you and not to harm you, plans to give you hope and a future'" (Jeremiah 29:11). He has a plan for you! You don't see it yet, but it's a great plan! It's prosperous, without harm, and has hope and a future! Cling to that promise. That's a great verse to memorize.

The problem with me telling you that you have purpose is that, if you're contemplating suicide, you're having difficulty surviving, let alone thriving. If you ever feel that low, please know there are people who love you, and you have other options. God loves you, and these feelings will pass. It may take time, but they will pass. I cannot emphasize enough that your hurt will ease. Please seek help. If you don't get the help you need, ask again. Ask someone else until you get the help you need. You could ask a trusted friend or adult, parent, aunt or uncle, teacher, preacher, or neighbor. If it's someone you trust and respect, they'll know how to get you help. May I suggest teachers if you're having trouble at school? They are wonderful people. Find one you like to confide in.

Death is final. Even though I believe in a glorious afterlife (if you are a Christian), I am glad I have experienced every part of this world and all it has to offer—the good, the bad, and the ugly. It will be perfect in Heaven for eternity. Life here on Earth is unique. Try to remember that life here will provide you with many different experiences, good and bad. Grasp all that life has to offer here and now. We only get this one chance, and even though it may not feel like it now, life passes quickly in the grand scheme of things.

I had a friend in high school who attempted suicide. She had moved away and attended a different school, so I didn't see her often. Afterward, she explained to me that she was feeling so depressed that she didn't even think about tomorrow. The only thing she could focus on was the deep sadness she was feeling in the moment. The sadness consumed her entirely.

If you're having suicidal thoughts, it's different from being in a rocky patch. I don't want to confuse difficult seasons with feelings of suicide. Suicidal thoughts are *not* part of that constant cycle of good and bad seasons; they are an extremely low point that most people never have to experience. So, if you are so sad that you don't want to go on, seek help immediately. It will eventually get better. *It always does.* Life has many highs and lows; that's part of what makes it so rare. Life has so many wonderful things to offer you if you stick around for them. My hope and prayer is for you to love your life.

My desire is that you are having fun, learning, and making great friends. That is truly wonderful if you are. If so, I would like to list the warning signs of suicide here so you can watch out for your **peers**, not only for your friends (medicinenet.com):

- withdrawal from friends and family members
- trouble in romantic relationships
- difficulty getting along with others
- changes in the quality of schoolwork or lower grades
- rebellious or risk-taking behaviors
- unusual gift-giving or giving away one's possessions
- appearing bored or distracted
- writing or drawing pictures about death
- running away from home

- changes in eating habits
- dramatic personality changes
- changes in appearance (for the worse)
- sleep disturbances
- drug or alcohol abuse
- talk of suicide, even in a joking way
- having a history of previous suicide attempts

These are signs of depression, which can lead to suicidal behavior:

- feeling sad, empty, or tearful nearly every day
- loss of interest in activities that were enjoyed in the past
- changes in eating and sleeping habits
- difficulty thinking and concentrating
- complaints of continued boredom
- complaints of headaches, stomachaches, or fatigue with no actual physical problems
- expressions of guilt and/or not allowing anyone to give praise or rewards

Verywellmind.com has some strategies to help start a conversation about suicide:

- Encourage them to describe what they're feeling. (Ex. "I had no idea things were so bad for you. What's going on?")
- Ask them to share whether a specific incident led to suicidal thoughts. (Ex. "What happened? I want to know more. It might help to talk about it.")
- Don't invalidate their feelings.
- Avoid saying things like "I think you're overreacting" or "You should appreciate all you have in life."
- Show acceptance.
- Listen without verbalizing judgment or disagreeing with their statements or feelings.

Once they have confided in you, here are more suggestions to offer them emotional support:

- Let them know you understand that they feel miserable.
- Remind them of your unconditional love.
- Let them know you are deeply concerned about their well-being.
- As compassionately as possible, let them know you do not want them to hurt themselves and you'll do anything to help them.
- Gently point out that suicide is not the solution. There are options to at least try.
- Promise to be there for them and to do whatever it takes to get them through this. Give reassurances of that.

Health.ny.gov also suggests the following:

- Do not ignore these warning signs.
- Talk openly with them and express concern, support, and love.
- Do not leave them alone.
- Remove harmful objects that could be used to harm them.
- Seek help immediately from a doctor, mental health services, emergency room, 9-1-1, or a suicide hotline. Suicide Hotline 9-8-8.

I also think it is important to notice the signs of bullying. These should be reported as well. There are three types of bullying (stopbullying. gov):

- Verbal bullying - teasing, name-calling, inappropriate sexual comments, taunting, threatening to case harm
- Social bullying - leaving someone out on purpose, telling other children not to be friends with someone, spreading rumors about someone, embarrassing someone in public
- Physical bullying - hitting/kicking/pinching, spitting, ripping/ pushing, taking or breaking someone's things, making mean or rude hand gestures

These behaviors are what cause many children to turn to suicide. Please help stop these behaviors. Reporting these behaviors can save a life. It may not be the popular thing to do, but it is the right thing to do.

FOOTPRINTS IN THE SAND

One night a man had a dream.
He dreamed he was walking along the beach with the Lord.
Across the sky flashed scenes from his life.
For each scene, he noticed two sets of footprints in the sand;
one belonging to him, and the other to the Lord.
When the last scene of his life flashed before him
he looked back at the footprints in the sand.
He noticed that many times along the path of his life
there was only one set of footprints.
He also noticed that it happened at the very lowest
and saddest times in his life.
This really bothered him, and he questioned the Lord about it.
"Lord, you said that once I decided to follow you,
you'd walk with me all the way.
But I have noticed that during the most troublesome times
in my life, there is only one set of footprints.
I don't understand why, when I needed you most, you would leave me."
The Lord replied, "My precious, precious child,
I love you and I would never leave you.
During your times of trial and suffering,
when you see only one set of footprints...
It was then that I carried you."

• • • Chapter 3 Questions • • •

1. When do you cry?

2. Have you ever had suicidal thoughts? Or do you know someone who has?

3. Have you noticed any of warning signs of suicide in your friends? If so, what did you do?

4. Do you have a specific memory you'd like to forget?

5. What Bible verse would you like to learn to repeat when you need instant encouragement?

6. What do you do when you're sad?

7. Ask several adults how often they think about their middle school or high school days.

Blessed is the one who perseveres under trial because, having stood the test, that person will recieve the crown of life.

James 1:12 NIV

If I can turn coal into diamonds, sand into pearls, and a worm into a butterfly, I can turn your life around too!

—God

CHAPTER 4

Love

• • • HUMANITY VS. FRIENDSHIP

Love is the greatest of all the commandments. To be honest with you, I would probably have a difficult time rattling off all of the Ten Commandments. There's always one or two I forget. My pastor once said something I love: Instead of remembering all ten, it's easier if you condense them to two—love God and love others. You should love God first and then love everybody else. Love is the most important thing we are called to do. If we can't do that, we cannot receive God's love.

When God tells us to love our fellow man, He's not only talking about love as a noun—the *thing* we feel toward our fellow human beings. He's mostly talking about love as a verb—an action we *do* for our fellow humans. We are to love everyone—our neighbors, family, friends, strangers, weak or strong—by serving them. There are no limits. Love others, even your enemies, by serving them. When you love others, you're loving God. This requirement from God is one of the things that sets Christianity apart from other religions.

My former school superintendent once said something about his secretary that I have always remembered. When he heard someone enter his office, he could never tell whether it was a parent, student, teacher, board member, or member of the community based on his secretary's response. She treated everyone with equal kindness and respect. What a compliment, and what a lady!

That's my hope for you. I want you to be kind to everyone. It doesn't matter what they look like, what position they hold, how much money they have, or how smart you think they are; just be kind to everyone. In fact, it's more important to be kind to those who are the lesser of these.

Some may advise you to be kind to everyone because you don't want to "burn any bridges." If you're cruel to someone, life has a way of nipping you in the behind. That very person you crossed may cross your path later on in life. They'll remember how you treated them. If you treated them poorly, most likely it won't go well for you. Although that may be *a* reason to be kind to everyone, it's not *the* reason. I want you to be kind to everyone because it's the right thing to do. Period. Just be kind.

If I had to give you one rule to live by, it would be very simple: Be kind. Be kind day in, day out to everyone—every body, every soul. Everyone. This simple rule will serve you well throughout your life.

Most people are easy to be kind to. But I know you know one or two people who might be a little difficult to love. Me too. We aren't perfect, are we? Some people just mesh easier with us than others. To be clear, we are still called to love them too, even the ones we don't feel connected to. I expect you to be kind to every human. You are not better than anyone else, and no one else is better than you. We're all here to live together as peacefully as we can. Do not discriminate or label others.

But there's a difference between being kind to everyone and choosing your friends. Being kind to everyone doesn't mean you have to be best friends with everyone. It really isn't that difficult to be cordial. It will not hurt you to smile and say hello. You do not have to have an in-depth conversation with everyone, but look them in the eye, smile, and speak. If you don't, it comes across as snobby. Please do not be a snob. (Snobs annoy me. Sometimes I can be judgmental, which is not of Christian character, and my judgment may or may not be accurate. I'm working on it.)

When in doubt, smile. A smile goes a long way. If you don't like something, smile and say "No, thank you." Or smile and say "Yes, please."

This is a very simple life lesson. Even if it's just in passing, look people in the eye, smile, and respond. This is a simple common courtesy I extend to fellow humans. (I also extend it to dogs, when appropriate.) As a Christian, I try to be kind to everyone. The adage "If you can't say anything nice, don't say anything at all" is as true today as it was when my grandparents said it. Here's another truth for you: The "don't say anything at all" part is very difficult. I'm still working on it. I have a couple really good friends I like to confide in. When we are talking with good friends, it is so easy to share not only our happy thoughts but also those thoughts that are not so…Christian-ish. Because we share *all* of us with our good friends, right? The good and the bad? We do it, but that doesn't make it right. Your mouth will get you in trouble. Be careful with conversations that start out with "Don't tell anyone, but…" or "Did you hear…?" or "Can you believe…?" There are many Bible verses warning us to watch that wagging tongue! Here's a couple of my personal favorites:

> "A gossip betrays a confidence; so avoid anyone who talks too much."
>
> Proverbs 20:19

> "Too much talk leads to sin. Be sensible and keep your mouth shut."
>
> Proverbs 10:19
(Is that clear enough?)

> "Everyone should be quick to listen, slow to speak, and slow to become angry."
>
> James 1:19

I advise you to learn the art of keeping confidences. We all want friends we can trust. It is a very honorable quality.

Likewise, be careful who you trust. Friends change rather quickly when you are young. Don't say or do anything that you wouldn't want posted publicly.

Many young people are suffering the ill effects of social media. I know it can be used in so many good capacities. Many experiences shared on social media are heartwarming and inspirational. That's wonderful if that has been your experience. Unfortunately, there's always going to be those who feel comfortable spreading hate and tearing others down behind a screen. I'm sorry if you've ever been the recipient of hurtful comments or worse. I'll be even sorrier if you're the one hurting others.

Stick up for others who need strength. Be a friend to them. Put yourself in their shoes. I try to live by the golden rule: "Do unto others as you would have done unto you." (Matthew 7:12) Treat others how you'd like to be treated. The world would be such a better place if everyone lived by this rule. (You can insert those rainbows and butterflies here.)

When Jesus came, he constantly spoke of loving others. "Above all, love each other deeply, because love covers over a multitude of sins" (1 Peter 4:8) This is comforting to me. If I love others, then my sins and imperfections will not be as significant in God's eyes. Loving other people is that important to Him.

Life isn't always black and white. Actually, I believe most of life is gray. At least for me it is. I hope I'm never chosen for jury duty; I can always see two sides to the story. As a teacher, I saw how most kids who were mean usually had a reason to act out. Not that it's okay to punch someone in the face just because you think you have a good reason. You always have a choice as to how you will respond in any situation. Violence is never the best choice. My experience has shown me that most children don't want to be mean or intentionally hurt others. There's always more to the story. My brother says there are three sides to every story: side one, side two, and the truth. Yes, there are some people who are evil and rotten. But I don't believe *most* people set out to see whom they can hurt today.

Try to surround yourself with friends who have Christian values, lofty goals, and kind hearts. They don't have to be exactly like you. It's great to have different kinds of friends. But you will be associated with the people you hang around. Make sure they represent you well. There are many Bible verses guiding us to surround ourselves with believers. 1 Corinthians 15:33 is one of many: "Do not be deceived: 'Bad company ruins good morals.'" It's important to have your friends be primarily Christians. There's strength in numbers. Once you start hanging out with other groups, or even spending too much time alone, Satan is so happy because then he has a higher chance of success in leading you astray. We're weaker when we try to do things alone or our own way.

Even as an adult, you have to worry about spending your free time with the right kind of people. What are their priorities or intentions in life? Are they genuine? Do they make you happier or a better person? Do they put you at ease to be yourself? Do you have common interests? Are they Christians?

I have friends who may not make decisions I agree with, but I will still be friends with them. I'm not going to stop being friends with them just because I believe they are making a mistake. God wants us to have Christians as our closest friends, but we should still be friendly with everyone. That is how you can show others God's goodness. When you really like a non-Christian, I think it's important to continue that friendship. You'll have an opportunity to share your faith with them.

However, if a friend brings me down spiritually or does something illegal or physically harmful, I would have to reconsider my friendship with them. It's a wonderful thing to support people and help them, and I'm not suggesting that you turn your back on them, but you can only do so much. They have to be responsible for their actions. You can't make them do or not do something. Do not make yourself responsible for the happiness or success of others. You don't have to fix the world. Be the best person you can be. Be responsible for you first as you love God and others.

You may not have the experience yet to be strong in your convictions. You're still figuring things out, and it's easy to be misled. Life is a series of choices, and the choices you make every day are significant. Obviously, I want you to make wise choices. Learn to pay attention to your feelings— when you're presented with a choice that makes the hair on the back of your neck stand up, or that little voice in your head says, "This probably isn't a good idea," or something simply makes you pause for a moment. Those signs should not be ignored, and you should take time to think through your actions. Don't let people pressure you for an immediate response. If they do, your response should be "No." Also, if you make a decision that you hope someone doesn't find out about, it's probably not a good decision.

When in doubt, be like Jesus. He had his twelve best friends, the apostles. They traveled as a group. But he didn't spend all his time only with them. He spent time with the poor, sick, outcasts, and lost souls. You don't have to save this world by yourself. Jesus can do that and did. Get a few, a couple, or even just one core good friend, and then be kind to everyone as a group. "Keep oneself from being polluted by the world." (James 1:27)

Being a quiet person, I didn't have much difficulty in school getting along with people, but I didn't have the social media you have now. Fortunately, I was unaware of what I was missing. I grew up on the "wrong side of the tracks." I definitely wasn't one of the cool kids, but I had a few friends that let me tag along at times. All you need is one good friend, and I did have that. (Thank you, Janelle.)

When my oldest went to high school, she struggled with finding a place to belong. She wasn't a social outcast or anything, but it was a small school, and she didn't seem to fit in with any of her peer groups. So she kept busy with soccer, her studies, reading, extra-curricular activities, clubs, and eventually a boyfriend. She got into a great college, which led to a great job. She was still figuring out her place in college. Once she started working and found her soulmate, she had many friends. Sometimes it just takes time. You will find your place.

My other daughter was a social butterfly, yet also struggled a couple times in high school and college. There was drama. There were a couple instances when kids were just downright mean and nasty. It was heartbreaking to watch her go through those times. Later, I found out things I didn't even know were going on, and I'm sure I still don't know the whole truth. She got through it, though, and even forgave them. I'm so proud of her for being such a forgiving soul. Mama Bear has a hard time forgiving those who hurt any of her cubs. It's very humbling when your child teaches you an important life lesson such as forgiveness. But as awful as it was for her to be the victim of cruelty, I'd rather her be a victim than a perpetrator.

Yes, kids can be mean. That doesn't mean that they will continue on that path when they're older and mature. The brain doesn't completely mature until the age of twenty-four. I found an article that explains how one of the areas of the brain that matures late is the prefrontal cortex; the area important in impulse control, risk-taking behavior, and judgment (sites.duke.edu). Read that last statement again. Impulses, risks, judgment—you are not mature until at least age twenty-four. Kids do stupid stuff. Sometimes they hurt people. It only takes one kid making bad decisions to make your life miserable. Try to have a forgiving heart. They are immature. Hang in there. It'll get better.

If it's happening to someone else, be the one that goes out of your way to be kind to those who are less fortunate. I realize that is asking a lot from you. It's not a popular choice. It may not make you popular, but it will make you a wonderful human being. Your character will become strong when you practice doing acts of kindness. You should start practicing right away. Even as an adult, it's important to look back and examine your reactions to decide if you helped or hindered in a given situation. That's not always easy to do amidst the drama, but try to. I've had to do some self-reflection a time or two.

Church

One way to make sure you have positive influences is to find a church where you feel comfortable. It can be a process. Churches are not perfect either. Sometimes I walk into church by myself, see all the perfect families, and start feeling a little anxious since I'm sometimes alone. This has become *my* insecurity. Those families are doing exactly what they should be doing—worshipping together. I tell myself that I am here to worship God; that is my priority. I will be faithful in worshipping Him no matter what self-doubt I place on myself. Worshipping takes precedence over my insecure feelings about belonging or sitting amongst families. I could easily use that as an excuse to not go to church, but I refuse to do that.

When my dad passed one Christmas, I went often to early church with my mom, which happens to be in the old church I grew up in. It's a very old beautiful church, a Lutheran church. There are things I get from worship there that I miss from my church. I miss kneeling to pray to God; I miss saying the Lord's Prayer; I miss stained glass windows, organ pipe music, ornate wood carvings, and pews; I miss the sacredness and holy feeling I get from worshipping God there; I miss the clergy in robes and some of the rituals. It emphasizes to me that I am in a holy place. For some reason, her church reminds me that God is omnipotent, that we are so unworthy, and that we are to bow down to His greatness. It brings to mind and makes me respect and cherish His divinity.

When I worship at my own church afterward, I feel the love of Jesus. I feel God's presence. The music there makes me feel closest to Him. At times, the music moves me to tears. People raise their hands rather than kneel to express their love. The message and feeling of God's love among the congregation is so great.

Two churches, two different feelings are evoked. Both have wonderful people, and both offer meaningful messages from the Word of God. One has an Old Testament "worship God" feel, the other a New

Testament "Jesus is love" feel. Choosing a church is an important step in your faith. Find a place where you feel you belong, where they are active in pursuing God's Word, and where you understand God's message so you can start living it. But remember: no church is perfect.

Recently, my husband found a church that is the perfect combination of both. I no longer sit alone. It's just right for us.

Some people don't go to church because they think Christians are all hypocrites. Technically, it is true. We are all sinners. I read somewhere once that church is not a house for saints; it's a hospital for sinners. Every one of us there is a sinner. You don't have to be perfect to be there.

Don't wait until you find the perfect place to worship God, or until you are perfect. That is never going to happen. At least the people attending church are there learning about God's Word. The trick is, when you leave church you have to then implement what you've learned. Loving God is a lifestyle, not a Sunday morning thing. When someone attends church and then continues to live in the same sinful manner, that turns people away from church and God. That person is a hypocrite.

You may hear of the adage: "Garbage in, garbage out." If you decide to fill your mind with garbage, that is what will come out of your mouth. Be in control of your mind. Try to use your private time to think happy or productive thoughts. If you decide to spend your time looking at porn or violent videos, listening to vulgar language or vulgar music, or spending time with people who like those things, that will eventually show in your actions or come out of your mouth. Evil can become etched in your brain and become part of your heart and soul just as easily as love. Belonging to a church makes it easier to fill your mind with good things.

Use the intelligence given to you for goodness. Don't fool yourself into thinking you can think one way and act another. It's just a matter of time before you'll implode. Control your thoughts. The devil is just waiting for your weakness so he can dwell. I will constantly remind you of this because it is very important. "Finally, brother, whatever is true, whatever is noble, whatever is right, whatever is pure, whatever is lovely, whatever is admirable—if anything is excellent or praiseworthy—think about such things" (Philippians 4:8).

There's another old saying: "Idle hands are the devil's workshop." I think this is true. It is best to be busy. Too much alone time is not healthy. What you do in your spare time will impact your daily living. If you choose to feed your mind garbage, you'll project garbage. Who you spend your time with has a huge impact on your personality and how you present yourself to the world. Choose your friends wisely. Surround yourself with people you'd want to emulate. Remember: garbage in, garbage out.

I'll leave you with one final "don't." Don't try to act one way around one set of friends and another way around other people. It is an impossible task to try to please everyone. Always be true to who you are. Be genuine with people. People can tell when you aren't. Be the wonderful person God made you.

> Friends pick us up when we fall, and if they can't pick us up,
> they lie down and listen for a while.
>
> —Unknown

> Friendship is like peeing in your pants. Everyone can see it,
> but only you can feel the warm feeling inside.
>
> —Robert Bloch

> Friends are people who know you really well and like you
> anyway.
>
> —Greg Tamblyn

> Love is blind. Friendship closes its eyes.
>
> —Friedrich Nietzsche

••• Chapter 4 Questions•••

1. Have you ever seen someone go out of their way to be kind? Have you ever gone out of your way to be kind?

2. Are you aware of the kind of people who mesh with you? What personality traits do you admire in your friends?

3. How often are you exposed to "garbage"?

4. Find another Bible verse about surrounding yourself with Christians.

5. Are you good at keeping secrets?

6. How can you build on a relationship with one of your peers?

7. Give some examples of how you love others.

8. Are most of your friends Christians?

9. Have you ever had to end a friendship?

10. Do you have someone you could share your faith with?

11. Have you ever sensed fear when making a decision?

12. Did you ever feel like you didn't belong?

13. Have you found a church where you're growing spiritually?

Therefore encourage one another and build one another up, just as you are doing.

1 Thessalonians 5:11

CHAPTER 5

Marriage

The single most important decision you'll make in your life is whether you will be a Christian. It may not seem like a big deal to you now, but your eternity depends on not only what you believe here and now but also how you respond to what you've been told.

The second biggest decision you'll make in your life is who you marry. I just explained to you how I think you should love your friends and fellow man. The love of your life is different. It should feel different.

Please don't think that since I've been married for over thirty years I'm going to be able to share the secrets to finding your perfect soulmate and keeping a perfect marriage. I think I got really lucky. Nah. I don't believe in luck. Since I'm a Christian, I have God guiding me.

I ponder what wisdom I have to guide you here. Part of me wants to provide you with a checklist: Does he do this? Does she do that? But feelings of love are more than a checklist. Chemistry is involved. It can't be explained on paper.

Maybe I could share how I want you to find that person you just *know* is *the one*. You don't want to think about your life without them. I could say that it should be an easy decision for you; if it's not easy, they are not the one. But it's not always that simple. No one is perfect. It's a big decision, so I think it's normal to be somewhat apprehensive to make that leap.

So maybe I could give you some characteristics that quality mates display. We usually want someone smart, kind, funny, attractive. That's pretty generic. People have different levels of all those attributes, and we attribute varying degrees of importance to them.

Let me give you some brief thoughts on each:

Smart—Let's try to go up in the gene pool.

Kind—It's a must. You decide the degree.

Funny—I love to laugh, but not all the time. You decide the degree. You've got to enjoy life though. I want you to be happy and have fun.

Attractive—Pretty is as pretty does. It would be nice to go up in the gene pool here too, but looks are not everything. I'd rather have the other three over looks. Some (definitely not all) people who look great can be high maintenance. It's better to find someone with a good heart. Once you really know someone, their attractiveness changes. If you choose someone solely on looks, you'll end up miserable. Mark my words! There must be more to your relationship than just looks.

I know there are many more attributes to consider. Make sure your potential mate already displays to some extent the attributes most important to you. This is not the time to choose a fixer-upper! Even by adolescence, personality traits are very difficult to change or learn. One study suggests that our personalities are set for life by first grade (livescience. com). If your potential mate does not have an attribute that is important to you now, chances are it will not suddenly appear one day.

Dating is practicing, discovering, and learning what you like and don't like in a mate. Remember, it's a process, and it takes time. I once heard a great sermon about being the person you are looking for (Bill Meaige, sermon). If you're looking for a smart, kind, funny, attractive person, then you should do your very best to be smart, kind, funny, and attractive. Be the kind of person you want to attract. Be a good catch for someone. I think that is great advice. Make sure you have your act together before you start involving someone seriously in your life, and don't get involved with someone whose life is a wreck. You should make *each other* better people. I repeat: This is not the time to choose a fixer-upper. That may sound harsh, but fixer-uppers will make your life so much harder.

How can I explain to you what true love should feel like? When you think you're in love, the idea of *true* love goes a step further. The Bible talks not only about loving your partner but also honoring and cherishing them. I think that's what sets apart a great love.

Do you feel honored and cherished? Do you want to spend the rest of your life honoring and cherishing this person? Do they put you first above all others at all times? Do you put them first above all others at all times? Your love should be obvious to other people. It's not enough to say the words and then not show it. Friends and family should be able to see that love. Listen to your loved ones' opinions, especially if you hear the same thing from more than one person. Your feelings are obviously the most important. I'm simply saying that if people you love and respect see the love or see some red flags, they should be seriously considered.

Once you have finally found that person—the love of your life, soulmate, can't-live-without-you person—congratulations! You're halfway there! Now, that person has to feel exactly the same way about you. That's the tricky part. It doesn't always work out that way. Sometimes love hurts. Getting a broken heart is all part of the process. It stinks and hurts like the dickens, but it means they are not your one. Allow yourself time to heal then try again.

It's been a long time since I made that important life decision thirty-plus years ago. I do remember some of the dating struggles we endured. I won't bore you with all my relationships, but I can share some of my personal experience of dating that led to marriage. Rusty and I met in college. We broke up three times before I figured out he was the one. The first time we broke up because, although I really liked him, he became a butthead who treated me poorly. I knew I deserved to be treated better, so I broke up with him, even though I really didn't want to.

The second time Rusty decided he had made a mistake and wanted me back, and I decided he needed to suffer longer so I continued to date around while stealing some midnight strolls with him around campus here and there. I didn't want to go running back to him. It's okay to have some self-respect.

We finally got back together, but I eventually broke up again. He was getting serious, and I knew I could not commit for life yet because I was still curious about other fish in the sea.

By my senior year of college we were engaged. He was a year ahead of me. He likes to tell people, "She broke up with me three times. I fixed her—I married her!" He always fought for me. I liked that.

There was one point where I could've gone another way, though. There was one guy I liked a lot who was very similar to me as far as our personalities go. In the end, I opted to go with the guy who was my opposite. Yes, opposites do attract.

Rusty and I are opposite in many ways. He likes to be busy all the time; I'm a homebody. He has a temper and has no problem with confrontation; I keep everything inside and try to be the peacemaker. He's very athletic; I'm not. He's a numbers man; I like to read. He takes risks; I'm practical and safe. He's competitive; I'm not. His personality has highs and lows; I'm pretty even keeled.

Even though much of our personalities are polar opposite, there are also many important traits that we have in common. We both believe in God and are Christians; we like to help people; we aren't extravagant in our wants; we believe in commitment and faithfulness; we enjoy life and like to have fun; we like to travel to some degree, but not extensively; family is important to us as well.

One of the reasons our marriage is successful is our core values are very similar. Personalities differ, but marriage is much easier if you have the same moral values. Our personalities are not so opposite anymore. We've both edged closer to the middle of the spectrum. For example, I voice my opinion more, and he doesn't fly off the handle as quickly. I believe we've made each other better people.

I heard this saying that resonated with me: "Women marry men thinking they'll change, and they don't. Men marry women thinking they'll never change, and they do." I do think I have changed the most. My husband has made me a lot stronger, yet I have softened him a little bit as well.

Once you've found that person who feels the same toward you, you're set, right? That's all you have to do? Wrong.

Marriage is not easy. We haven't had many major problems other than a health scare when our son was born. We manage our money; our children have been respectful and hard-working; our families all get along; life has been wonderful. And yet, marriage is still hard. Friends of ours have a sign in their home that says, *I love you more today than yesterday... because yesterday you really ticked me off!* Some days marriage is like that.

We've obviously had many more good days than bad. I just don't want to mislead you into thinking that if you find the right person your married life will be easy. You will have hurdles. Circumstances change and people change, so make sure you have someone who values commitment.

Also, it's important to note that there are different stages of love. It's so wonderful at the beginning with the butterflies and can't-get-enough-of-each-other stage. That's phase one. It ends. If you only love that phase, you're not ready for commitment.

The more you get to know your partner, the deeper your feelings will be. Learning all about them is phase two.

Once you know them, you get comfortable with this understanding. You become familiar with each other, easing into a routine because you know each other's expectations. This is phase three.

The next phases are commitment and marriage, then sharing your body, experiencing the birth of a child, and making life decisions together. Your phases are going to vary, but that is how it happened for me. Yes,

I just made those phases up. They were all wonderful, beautiful phases. They intertwine, and each requires communication; perhaps disagreements occur, which leads to compromise. All the while you are proceeding through life together, growing in your love. It goes so fast!

As irritating as Rusty can sometimes be (and I can be as well), I do have difficulty picturing my life without him. I've been with him two-thirds of my life now. I can be routine and boring if you'll let me. He challenges me and makes me stronger. We've been through a lot of life together. I am better because of him.

Your love grows deeper. It evolves. Don't expect the butterflies to last. I suppose it does for some people, but I don't think that's the norm. That isn't a bad thing. Love changes as you learn to depend on each other and take care of each other. It's a different feeling than butterflies. It's warmth and security. It's knowing that someone is there for you. It's a wonderful thing to have a partner you can depend on. As you age, love deepens. It's important to continue to honor and cherish your spouse through the aging process. It's easy to fall into a comfort zone, which can easily lead to neglectfulness.

Once you start doing life—taking care of the kids, working all day, running kids around, fixing dinner, helping with homework, taking a bath, cleaning the house, paying some bills—I don't know where the time went! I retired six years ago, looked around, and there were no kids to shuttle or worry about, except for the normal worries that come with being a parent at any age. They were on their way to independent lives. I no longer had to worry about how to help my students or what new approach to use in teaching. I had all this time, and I looked at this man whom I would now be spending more time with.

Honestly, I wasn't sure I was happy with where we had landed. I feared we were on our way to becoming that old, crabby, bickering couple. How did that happen? We were lacking in the honoring and cherishing department. There was always love, but we somehow were losing the appreciation for each other. I did not want to spend the last chapter of our lives going down that path. I refused to choose that path. Maybe it was menopause. My hormones may have been out of whack. Call it what you want, but I decided there needed to be a change, or a boost, or something.

I decided to seek Christian counseling for some outside perspective and unbiased insight. We talked about things like boundaries, levels of intimacy, communication, and how if you aren't swimming forward, you're drifting backward. If you aren't growing, you're dying—you get the picture. We had found the right person but weren't putting the work into the relationship to keep it strong and thriving. We had been treading water or drifting backward for a while. We got too comfortable. So we did the work, made some adjustments, and are back on track again. I am so much happier again.

Work on your marriage every day. Don't ignore your feelings. Deal with issues as they arise, which is difficult for me as someone who wants to be a peacemaker. My new rule I learned from my counseling is that you have twenty-four hours to get it off your chest. I've heard some couples say you should never go to bed angry. I guess it's best to stay up and fight? Seriously, address your issue in a respectful and timely manner.

Before I started this chapter, I asked Rusty to list ten things he loved about me and five things he didn't love. I did the same for him. This exercise reminded us why we still love each other. It also served as a reminder that you have to take the good with the bad. Even after thirty-plus years of marriage, there's room for improvement.

I do think opposites attract. As I mentioned earlier, Rusty's personality challenges me. He is not boring. I also love how he takes care of people, his intelligence, confidence, energy, and generosity. The part I could do without is his brutal honesty. His, "If you're going to do it, do it right!" mentality and roller-coaster personality are also taxing.

Rusty loves me mostly for my stable personality. Again, I think I provide the calm to his storm. He says I am caring, uncomplaining, and conscientious of spending. I'm a great mother and I take care of myself.

Apparently, I need to improve on my confidence. I am too sensitive, sometimes I assume too much, and I need to learn to let out that anger!

I find it interesting that the qualities we love about each other are also the qualities that sometimes drive us a little crazy. For example, I love his zest for life, but it can be tiring. Sometimes I have to remind myself, "You are not lazy. You're normal. He's a bit over the top." He loves my caring and nurturing nature, but he wishes I just told him when I'm mad instead of bottling it up inside. He also says I can't take a compliment, and I say he needs to learn how to give a compliment.

That's us after thirty-four years of marriage. It's obvious that communication is an important factor we need to continue to improve upon. See? Marriage is not easy. Make sure both you and your partner value the sanctity of marriage. There will be difficult days.

Depending on where you are in life, you may not be thinking about marriage yet, but I'm not planning on doing a sequel, so I have to cram it all in this one book.

I cannot let you make the second biggest decision of your life without reminding you that it is important to take everything to God in prayer. And this is a big one. I want you to feel God's approval of your mate. I'd even pray about who you should date. He'll put people in your life for various reasons. Sometimes it's to help you learn what you don't want in a partner.

Do I believe everyone has one soulmate? I do not. I believe that, like in all aspects of our lives, God gives us free choice. This is no different. You get to choose, then God will do His work from there *if* you have Him in your life. I do believe some choices are better than others, and I want you to make the best choice.

Often people don't consult God first, choose a mate themselves, get married, and then discover it wasn't the right person. The marriage wasn't intended by God to begin with. I wonder how many times people choose themselves and then cry to God when the marriage is a disaster. That doesn't mean God can't or won't work in that marriage, but that's doing life the hard way. Your life will be blessed if your marry the right one to begin with. You will be blessed especially if you're on the same Christian path. (Chapter 13 discusses the four ways God will speak to you after you pray.)

Faithfulness is another important trait, even in dating. If they cheat while you're dating, don't be surprised if they cheat when you're married. That's not true for everyone, but it is an indicator for many. Once a cheater, always a cheater? Research from psychologytoday.com says that "those who were unfaithful in one relationship had three times the odds of being unfaithful in the next, when compared to those who had not been unfaithful in the first relationship."

Rusty and I have always said that if one of us cheats, it's over. We still feel that way today. Once the trust is broken, I have no desire to work on the marriage. (Forgiveness: I'm working on it. Boy, that list is getting long. Be patient; God's not done with me yet.) My argument is, being married to such a busybody, I would refuse to spend my time constantly checking up on him or wondering where he is or was since the trust would be broken. I choose not to live that way. I would not be a happy person.

That doesn't mean everyone else feels that way. I know of marriages that were broken but strengthened because of the love and forgiveness one partner granted. That's a lot of heartache, brokenness, distrust, and then work to rebuild a marriage, with feelings of anger, bitterness, and sadness. It's a lot to go through. Don't do that to someone you love, have loved, or even dated. Be an honorable person.

Obviously, abuse should never be tolerated. Get out and seek help immediately. Addictions—that's a tough one. I would do everything I could, including Christian counseling and a lot of prayer. But at the end of the day, I'm not sure I could stay in a marriage and be miserable. How sad it would be to love someone and then watch them be so out of control. I would pray, pray, pray, and listen to God. He will lead you.

It's difficult for me to sit here and say that you should do this and you should do that. I can't judge and tell you what to do because I do not have all the information. Every situation and person is different. I don't know what I'd do until I'm actually in that situation. If I haven't been in your shoes, I can't tell you what is best. *Get Christian counseling.* That's the best advice I can give you.

I will share this with you: I believe you should date someone at least six months before you marry them. I've heard that people can't hide their "crazy" that long. Do not rush into marriage. I advise at the very least a year of dating, preferably two. Once you learn all about your significant other's vices and imperfections (because we all have them), and you love them *happily* anyway, that's a good sign you are in love. On the other hand, if their imperfections and vices get on your nerves, it will probably not be a long-lasting love.

I come from a family of strong Christian women. My mom was raised going to church but really turned to God when she had to deal with being married to an alcoholic. She jumped into Christianity with both feet. God answered her prayers of sobriety for my dad eighteen years later. My mom insisted I go to college so I'd never be dependent on a man; she felt trapped since she was unable to support her children alone. Take it from my mom: Be independent! I do love the fact that I do not need a man in order to survive. If something had happened in our marriage, that would not have been an issue for me. Thanks, Mom.

My mom is a rock! She is a spiritual inspiration and my friend. Usually when I stop by to see her, she is curled up on the end of the couch reading her Bible. She is constantly reading God's Word. That's how I'll always picture her. (I also love it when she gets the giggles. It's infectious.)

I am also considered the religious one in our family. Rusty's mother, Libby, was the religious leader in their home. My tender-hearted sister-in-law is also the religious leader in her home. My dad and Rusty's dad became Christians toward the end of their lives. Women, I pray you find a Christian man to walk together with God right from the beginning. He will bless your marriage. If you choose not to do marriage that way, then you can be an example and do your best to guide your family. That's doing life the hard way.

Men, I pray for you to be the leader in your home by following God. It's time for the men to step it up! That is a gift you will give your family that will be everlasting. There's nothing greater you could do for yourself and them. Strong, godly men are so attractive and quite a catch! It is not common these days. You would be unique. Find yourself a good Christian woman so you can build a life together looking to Jesus Christ as your model.

> "We are all a little weird, and life's a little weird, and when we find someone whose weirdness is compatible with ours, we join up with them and fall in mutual weirdness, and call it love."
> —Dr. Seuss

> "If you want something to last forever, you treat it differently. You shield it and protect it. You never abuse it. You don't expose it to the elements. You don't make it common or ordinary. If it ever becomes tarnished, you lovingly polish it until it gleams like new. It becomes special because you have made it so, and it grows more beautiful and precious as time goes by."
> —F. Burton Howard

THE WRONG WISH

A married couple, both sixty years old, were celebrating their thirty-fifth anniversary. During their party, a fairy appeared to congratulate them and grant them each one wish.

The wife wanted to travel around the world. The fairy waved her wand and *poof!* The wife had tickets in her hand for a world cruise.

Next, the fairy asked the husband what he wanted.

He said, "I wish I had a wife thirty years younger than me."

So, the fairy picked up her wand and *poof!* The husband was ninety!

• • • CHAPTER 5 QUESTIONS • • •

1. Have you felt like you've been in love yet?
2. What is the difference between love and a crush or infatuation?
3. What are some qualities you are attracted to in a potential mate?
4. What are some signs of love you see in others?
5. Define *honor* and *cherish*. What is the difference?
6. Have you ever made a decision and wished you had prayed about it first?
7. Have you ever had to forgive someone for something?
8. What could you never tolerate from a partner?
9. Do you know a strong Christian man? Woman? Couple?

Be devoted to one another in love. Honor one another above yourselves.

ROMANS 12:10

CHAPTER 6

Sex

No one wants to talk with their grandma about sex. Believe me, I'm not thrilled with it either, but here we go. I'm going to assume you know all about the birds and the bees. Don't fret, I'm not going into those details. Prepare yourself for my old-fashioned, Bible-following advice.

Sex is a gift from God to be experienced between a husband and a wife. That's it. It's a beautiful thing that is very personal. We should treat it as a gift and something that is of great value. You have to regard it highly. It will not be special if you don't make it special.

Many people don't treat it like it's special because they prefer instant gratification. They do not treasure the gift and simply see sex as a thing that feels good. They see it as a physical need. Others view it as an emotional connection. It's used by others as a symbol of where they are in a relationship. I'm sure there are other reasons. All of these are wrong. Sex is only to be shared between a husband and wife. It's a way to express your love. It's a gift.

Since this is a topic that many young people dive right into, I want to be sure you have thought about the consequences of acting too soon, so you can consider saving yourself for marriage.

I'm going to assume that this other person is telling you that they love you and they are ready to take the next step with you. There is no next step you can take as a couple that will take your relationship deeper. Your body is the most personal thing you can share with another human being. You will be sharing the most intimate part of you. It is the ultimate prize you have to offer someone. When you give your body, you are giving them everything; you'll have nothing of higher value to offer, nothing still sacred about yourself.

I want you to view yourself as a prize. You are special. Every person that you date is not worthy of experiencing every part of you there is to offer—even if that person says they love you. Saying it does not make them worthy of all of you. Hold yourself as an ultimate prize to be won by someone deserving of you. "...We are the clay, you are the potter; we are all the work of your hand." (Isaiah 64:8) If you don't want to honor your body for God, at least honor your body for yourself. This is the one area in life where I want you to be **extremely selfish.**

I repeat: Treat yourself as a gift to be treasured. If you do not treat yourself that way, no one else will either. Hold yourself to high standards and have high expectations. You deserve that. Again, be selfish. Giving of yourself is all about you. If you aren't married, then I don't care *what* the other person's feelings are.

High School Sweethearts

Maybe you're thinking that this person is *the* one. Reality is, the chances of you marrying (and staying married to) your high school sweetheart are low. According to mensdivorce.com, Brandon Gaille Marketing found, "Divorce rates for those within the first ten years of marriage for a high school sweetheart were at 54 percent and were much higher than the average American couple at 32 percent; and only 2 percent of marriages today are from a high school relationship." Therefore, if you give yourself to someone in high school, chances are extremely high that you will *not* end up with this person for life. I urge you to reconsider giving your most precious gift to someone that you will likely never marry. Who deserves your gift? Your husband or wife does. You are a prize not to be shared with a first love, childhood sweetheart, crush, or fling. Don't minimize your gift.

Here are some more statistics from nwitimes.com:

- 54% of teenagers wish they had waited until they were older.
- 71% of girls said they were in love with their last sexual partner; 45% of the boys said the same. (Ladies, this statistic is *very* telling.)
- 81% of boys said sex is a pleasurable experience; 59% of the girls said the same. (Ladies, this statistic is *very* telling as well.)
- 75% of teenagers having sex said they were using birth control always or most of the time. (This statistic needs to be a lot better.)
- 14% said they did not use a condom all or most of the time to prevent AIDS or other sexually transmitted diseases. (Again, much room for improvement.)

MAKING THE DECISION

I was a virgin when I married. Even back then that was not common. This sex stuff has been going on for a long time! There's nothing new that God hasn't seen before. What if you don't find anyone into your twenties and thirties? I know: "You have needs." If you haven't found the right person, are you supposed to wait forever? I'm saying God will bless you if you do.

On a few occasions, when I dated someone for awhile, I was always honest and forthcoming that I was saving myself for marriage. If he was honorable enough, he would help me attain that goal. If he didn't stick around, I knew he wasn't looking for love. I saved myself a lot of heartache and time by saving myself. The heartache stings after a breakup, but it's so much easier when you don't get more emotionally involved by sharing your body. The closer you are in the relationship, the harder the breakup will be. Regular breakups are hard enough.

When I hear of kids who become sexually active at a young age, I am saddened. I don't want you to think, "I'm just going to wait until I'm in the moment and see if it feels right." This is not a decision to be made "in the moment." This is a decision you need to think about when you are alone and have all of your brain cells focused on the pros and cons. So many people make the decision right then and there without thinking through the consequences, and then they aren't prepared. The consequences can be life-changing. There are many for you to consider: guilt, shame, and embarrassment, to name just a few emotional consequences. Physical consequences can be just as damaging when you consider the possibility of STDs or an unwanted pregnancy. Some of these can be lifelong. Others may be temporary, but they'll still leave scars that will hinder you in future relationships.

Keep something about you out of reach. You will be remembered more for the "no" decision than if you concede. Be the one that got away. Be unique. Be respected. You'll be remembered for that.

I know it makes me sound like an old fuddy-duddy. I dated some pretty wonderful guys, but there's not one that I wish I'd experienced that first time with above my husband.

It's difficult to deal with this issue of being dumped afterwards. I know what you're thinking. "They would never do that to me. They love me!" They probably are a nice person. Or they love you until there's someone who looks better or just different, or they're bored with you, or curious about another, or any multitude of reasons. Here's another harsh reality: *This is to be expected* because dating is a process to help you find your true one. *Jumping into a sexual relationship does not make that person any more right for you.* If they are not the one, there will eventually be some reason for the break up. It's just a matter of time. Or, don't be surprised if it's you who suddenly or gradually feels differently. Your hormones at this stage of life are raging. It is normal for teenagers to experience changes in behavior and emotions (archives.drugabuse.gov).

PEOPLE ARE LIKE SHINY APPLES

This reminds me of a book I used to read to my kids when they were little, *The Berenstain Bears Learn About Strangers* by Stan and Jan Berenstain. They use the analogy of eating an apple: Sometimes you see a pretty red apple that looks delicious and then, occasionally, when you bite into it, the inside is rotten. People can be like that. Most people are pretty and wonderful and their insides are too. But every once in a while you'll run into one that is rotten inside. You simply can't tell just by looking. The moral of the story is to beware of strangers because most people are great, but every once in a while you find one that's rotten inside. And you can't tell that by looking at them.

I am giving you the same warning for dating. Most people you date are going to be wonderful and genuine. But you really can't tell for sure until you get to know them—or after the breakup. That's when true colors come out. If you've given all of yourself already, it's too late. Your mending process will be harder. It's not the end of the world, but why would you put yourself through that? That's doing life the hard way.

There's a hidden benefit to making your intentions of waiting known. Once you get that reputation, certain guys or gals won't consider dating you—which is a blessing, I might add. It weeds out the rotten ones! Girls, do not let a guy pressure you into sex. If he really cares about you, he will stick around. If he doesn't stick around, he's not the one. Save yourself the heartache. The guilt. If you do have sex and then wish you hadn't, that's not rape—that's regret. Be mad at yourself, not him/her. (I pray you never have to experience rape.) Once you've given yourself, you can never go back. Be in control of your body and your decision. Once you give of yourself like that, you no longer have that pure piece of yourself to offer your husband or wife.

YOU ARE A BEAUTIFUL ROSE

You may have heard the analogy that giving yourself is like a beautiful rose: For every person you have sex with, you're giving away a petal of your rose. When you have sex with a lot of people, you're eventually left with a stick! Sex won't be anything special because you've shared it with so many people.

You have to make it special. If a guy won't wait for you, he doesn't love you. The guy who loves you will do anything for you. I love it when Steve Harvey shares with women exactly how guys are. I think of him as a spy that we have on the inside. He tells us exactly what men are thinking and what they want. He states it pretty simply: "If you're the one, we will do anything for you." So, if you're not being treated the way you think you should, then he's just not that into you. The man who loves you will do anything for you. Wait for the person who will honor and cherish you. You deserve that.

Please know how valuable and wonderful you are. Save yourself for someone who is deserving of you. Know your worth. God Himself says you are worthy! "For you created my inmost being; you knit me together in my mother's womb. I praise you because I am fearfully and wonderfully made; your works are wonderful, I know that full well." (Psalm 139:13-14)

Men, you also are very special. I am talking to you too about keeping sex sacred. I know it's just as hard for you to wait. People don't expect abstinence anymore. Our society is so flippant about sex. I hope you will hold your body in high regard as well, and it is my hope for you to be pure at your marriage. Sex is something to discover with your spouse. Having self-control and high standards makes you unique and a great catch.

Find the woman you want and treat her better than you do yourself, always. Put her needs above yours. Is she someone you would lay your life down for? Is she someone you want to take care of? Does she have a kind heart? Looks are not everything, but do you think she's beautiful? Every once in a while, tell her so. Girls like to be told they're pretty. Do you love her enough to cherish and honor her above all others? For life?

Remember when I told you, "Pretty is as pretty does?" She may be pretty on the outside, but if her heart is not kind, over time you won't even think she's pretty on the outside. (Think of that red apple.) Likewise, someone may not look so great, but as you get to know them they become very attractive to you. Give everyone a chance. Don't judge by looks! Know their heart. "Charm is deceptive, and beauty is fleeting; but a woman who fears the Lord is to be praised." (Proverbs 31:30) This goes for women too.

Oopsies

Let's say there was an oops. Things got out of control. Women, if you do get pregnant, in my opinion, there are only two options. I strongly urge you to raise your baby if at all possible. *Children are such a blessing*, but it's harder when you aren't married, educated completely, employed, or living independently. It will be easier if you are in a loving relationship with your spouse. Yes, life will be harder, but a child will bring you so much joy.

Men, if you get in this situation, don't be a deadbeat dad. My expectation for you would be to have the baby, love him/her, and raise that child as a Christian with Christian values. If you mess around, be prepared to deal with the consequences. Be there physically, financially, emotionally, and all the other ways you need to be for a child you helped to create. The statistics for children without fathers are eye-opening: they are more likely to end up in poverty or drop out of school, become addicted to drugs, have a child out of wedlock, or end up in prison (all4kids.org). The father is just as important as the mother in the life of a child.

The second option is adoption. Some of the unsung heroes in our country are women and men who give their babies up for adoption rather than choose abortion. So many couples have difficulty having children and would love to have that baby. Rusty and I sponsor a child in Colombia. I love knowing that we make a difference in someone's life on another continent that we don't even know. My soul is happy that I'm helping a stranger. I realize this is only a small fraction of the emotion involved when you give away your child, but adoption is one of the most loving acts you could ever do. What a gift!

Those are your two choices: keep the baby or adoption. My hope and prayer for you is that abortion is never an option. Abortion is not birth control. Do not punish your unborn child for your mistakes. There are plenty of people who would love to take that child for you and love it if you can't or won't. Give that baby a chance.

Too embarrassing? Don't want to ruin your body? Your image? Don't have nine months to go through all that? You have other plans for your life? It would bother you to have a life you created out there living in the world? I hate to tell you this, but those excuses are all selfish. I know the argument: it's your body, your life, your choice. What about the body, life, choice of the baby? Those don't count? It's not really a life? If it's not a life, why does it have to be killed? Find a video of an abortion and watch it. I've seen one, and I couldn't bring myself to watch it again. That baby did nothing wrong. This is not an acceptable alternative. It's cruel. If you want free choice, once you decide to become sexually active, you can decide which method of birth control you want to use. There's your free choice. There are many options.

In the US, there are over 3,000 abortions *per day* (worldometers. info). Nearly half of all pregnancies are unintended, and four in ten are terminated by abortion. A staggering 22% of all pregnancies in the USA (excluding miscarriages) end in abortion. Ladies and Gents, we have got to be better than that. We're smarter than that. This statistic is loathsome.

Sorry, I know this is a touchy subject, but if you aren't going to wait to have sex until marriage, you must get on birth control. No excuses. Be better than the statistics. Use birth control and use it right.

And if all this isn't enough to reconsider being sexually active before marriage, then Google images of STDs. I'm not even going to go into how nasty people can be physically. According to cdc.gov, they estimate that on any given day in 2018, one in five people in the US had a sexually transmitted infection (STI). Some people don't even know they have an

STI because the symptoms are slight or nonexistent. However, if they go untreated, there can be long-term problems, which may include pelvic pain, pregnancy complications, eye inflammation, arthritis, pelvic inflammatory disease, infertility, heart disease, or certain cancers (mayoclinic. org). Do not gloss over this list and think it won't happen to you. It can, and it is very possible.

As I read over this chapter, it sounds a little negative. I don't mean to be. I don't think you want to hear Grandma go into details about how great sex is either. I simply want to make sure that you realize that sex is a beautiful gift from God to be experienced between a husband and wife. Teenagers are not mature enough to make these kinds of decisions and then deal with the emotional ramifications of a failed relationship, let alone more difficult consequences like STDs or unwanted pregnancy. I am all for enjoying the gifts from God as God intended for them to be enjoyed.

••• Chapter 6 Questions •••

1. Do you know anyone who has had sex and regretted it?
2. Will you consider saving yourself for marriage?
3. Do you think you are a prize?
4. Do you have access to birth control? Discuss this with your parents.
5. Can you offer some advice on breakups?
6. What traits would make one a "rotten shiny apple?"
7. What are your thoughts on abortion?
8. List 5 STDs:

   1.

   2.

   3.

   4.

   5.

For this very reason, make every effort to supplement your faith with virtue, and virtue with knowledge, and knowledge with self-control, and self-control with steadfastness, and steadfastness with godliness, and godliness with brotherly affection, and brotherly affection with love. For if these qualities are yours and are increasing, they keep you from being ineffective or unfruitful in the knowledge of our Lord Jesus Christ.

2 Peter 1:5-8 ESV

CHAPTER 7

Gifts

The fruits of the Holy Spirit are love, joy, peace, patience, kindness, goodness, faithfulness, gentleness, and self-control. You will recieve these gifts once you become a Christian and have the Holy Spirit in you.

After a serious chapter of sex talk, let's move on to a lighter subject: your gifts.

Your Gifts Are Like the Sprinkles on a Sugar Cookie

We all have been blessed with some talent (that's the extra dash God put on your cookie). It can be so many things: musical ability, athletic ability, getting along with people, making people laugh, teaching, listening, leading, intelligence, healing, building things, tearing things down, redoing things, multitasking, physical fitness, cooking, writing, reporting, decorating, organizing, drawing, dancing, artistic ability. I can't list them all. Some people are blessed with multiple gifts.

Find your gifts and use them. You are given these gifts to bless others. If you don't use your gifts, God will want to know why you didn't use them. "From everyone who has been given much, much will be demanded; and from the one who has been entrusted with much, much more will be asked." (Luke 12:48) Your gifts may not only be talents but possibly wealth, knowledge, or time.

Over the years, I have discovered my gifts. I am not super talented in any one area. You did not receive any superpower genes from me. But I do have some skills! I think the biggest gift God decided to bless me with is my patience. I can also get along with just about anybody. These two gifts were especially useful as a teacher working with children with disabilities. In addition, I am a peacemaker. I try to do what is needed to make everyone happy. Some may not consider that a gift. I do.

I think overall, I'm pretty average, except for my patience, friendliness, and peacekeeping skills. Those are the sprinkles on my sugar cookie. The other gifts I have are just part of who I am. I can sort of carry a tune and read music from playing piano as a child; I can water ski and snow ski (though I have to work at it because sports don't come naturally to me); I'm not very funny, but I love to laugh; I love to work (I also love to chill, I just can't do it day after day); I'm not beautiful, but I'm not ugly; most people would say I'm a happy person, I think; I'm not brilliant, but I'm not stupid. I told you it wasn't anything amazing, but I choose to be happy with what God gave me. While my cookie could be a lot better, it sure could be a lot worse. Thank you, Lord, for the gifts you gave me.

As you grow and experience things, you'll find your gifts. Hopefully, you'll find a profession that is conducive to using them, that lets you shine. I know you will make a difference in this world. It doesn't matter what profession you choose; God will use you to do His will wherever you are. But using your God-given talent will make your job easier and more enjoyable. And when you use your gifts every day, you'll become exceptional in that area.

If you don't use your talent in your job, make sure you use it in other ways: at church, volunteering, in hobbies or activities, and in your relationships. Your talents are not given to you to make you look great. They are given to you so you can serve others. Remember, we love God by loving and serving others. Use your gifts.

Whatever you decide to do, choose a vocation that makes you happy. My husband and I always told our children, if you can't speak highly of where you are working, then don't work there anymore. Move on. When you are working and serving, be happy. God loves a cheerful giver—give of yourself, your time, and your money. "Each of you should give what you have decided in your heart to give, not reluctantly or under compulsion, for God loves a cheerful giver." (2 Corinthians 9:7)

Music

If you have been blessed with even a dash of musical talent, I am a little envious. The ability to sing, play, compose, dance, choreograph, write, or mix music is a God-given talent. You have been truly blessed. Even though I'm not blessed extensively in this area, I'm so glad there are others who are.

I love the feelings music brings to any occasion. I can't imagine this world without it. Music is powerful! How dreary would life be without it? There simply are no words that adequately describe its effects on us.

If someone believes the Earth was created accidentally, as well as man and woman, then I'm sure they would not think the creation of music is anything miraculous. But I do. It brings people joy every day.

Music sets the tone at events: the band at a football game, soft sounds at a spa, weddings, funerals, parties, beach music, jazz, oldies night, classical, old hymns, country, rock, tailgate, musicals—I love it all! Okay, maybe I don't love absolutely every kind of music, but I do love a lot of different kinds of music. I truly respect every kind of music because it evokes all kinds of feelings and has the power to soothe the soul, heal hearts, motivate, calm, celebrate, and just have fun. I love how a song can bring back memories of a special place or event.

Hans Christian Andersen said, "Where words fail, music speaks." Music adds emotion to all of life's experiences, good and bad. Bryce W. Anderson says, "I've found that no matter what life throws at me, music softens the blow." Life is definitely enhanced at all levels with music. It makes life richer and more meaningful. "Music is the ultimate adornment to our gift of life." Penny Deaton.

Music is referenced in Bible verses over 1,150 times (insearchoftruth. org). God loves music. I must admit that I feel closest to God when I'm singing Him praises. Sometimes it moves me to tears. I don't want you to think that God *only* loves those beautiful church hymns or the wonderful praise songs, although I'm sure they must be His favorites. I think God loves all kinds of music. Don't put God in a box and think of Him only inside a church building. I'll bet He taps His toes or goes full out dancing to many beats. I wonder if Heaven will have instruments that we haven't experienced yet? Maybe he has some special sounds only to be experienced there.

I did learn how to play the piano when I was young, so I have the basic knowledge of reading music. I was not a prodigy in any area. Dancing came easier to me than playing the piano, and I wish I had placed practicing the piano higher on my list of priorities. Learning how to read music has been a blessing I've enjoyed all my life. There are many benefits to playing an instrument, such as it reduces stress, cultivates creativity, uses almost every part of the brain, benefits spelling and IQ in children, strengthens your immune system, and there are many more benefits (pianopower.org).

Good news for me: "A growing number of studies show that music lessons in childhood can do something perhaps more valuable for the brain than childhood gains: it provides benefits as we age in the form of an added defense against memory loss, cognitive decline, and diminished ability to distinguish consonants and spoken words (api.nationalgeo-graphic.com)." Yes, I do wish I had stuck with the piano. Music will be a part of your life forever. You will determine how so. I strongly encourage that if you are given the opportunity, learn how to play an instrument. You won't regret it.

Also, try different things so you can find out what your gifts are. You never know until you try! Of course, I'm not talking about only the stereotypical activities. Try it all! Playing sports also teaches many valuable life lessons. Sports were not encouraged for me in my growing-up years, but all our children played sports and a musical instrument at some point. We always believed it was best to expose our children to many different activities, so they could find out not only what they enjoy, but also what their gifts were. Be active. There are so many opportunities and experiences available. See what comes naturally to you.

Even when you are blessed with a talent, it still requires hard work to become exceptional in that area. I don't want to give you the impression that you never have to work at something you're talented in. All of the greats practice hard.

Music is a language to your soul. Even though it's a universal language, it is very personal in the way it touches your soul. I want you to know that when I die I'll be singing my praises to the Lord, my Savior, in a deep, throaty, powerful voice like Christina Aguilera. I'm going to sound awesome! I sound good now when I'm in my car by myself, but you're just going to have to trust me on that one (wink).

•••Chapter 7 Questions•••

1. What are your gifts? Do you have multiple gifts?

2. What music do you enjoy?

3. Share a music quote you can relate to.

4. How are you a cheerful giver?

5. When I hear the song _____, it reminds me of the time...

6. What instrument do you play or would like to play?

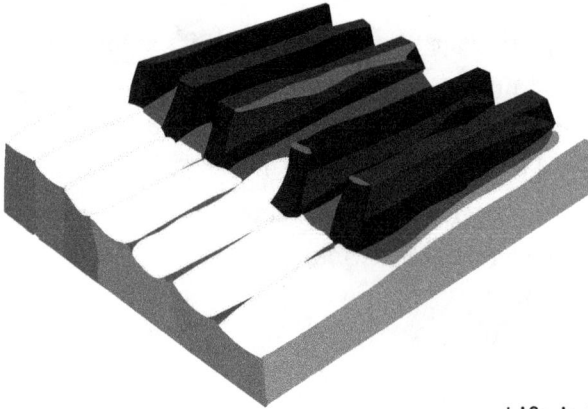

Life is like a piano;
white keys are the happy moments,
and black keys are the sad moments.
Both keys are played together
to give us the sweet music called Life.

Suzy Kassem

God has given each of you a
gift from his great variety
of spiritual gifts. Use them well
to serve one another.

1 Peter 4:10 nlt

CHAPTER 8

Happiness

· · · · ·

"Most comedy is based on getting a laugh at somebody else's expense. And I find that that's just a form of bullying in a major way. So I want to be an example that you can be funny and be kind, and make people laugh without hurting somebody else's feelings."

—Ellen DeGeneres

This is in contrast to this quote:

"It's always funny until someone gets hurt. Then it's just hilarious."

—Bill Hicks

...which leads me to the conclusion:

"What a strange world this would be if we all had the same sense of humor."

—Bernard Williams

So, I'll agree with Dr. Seuss:

"From there to here, and here to there, funny things are everywhere."

—Dr. Seuss

One of the gifts I mentioned in the previous chapter is a sense of humor. The ability to make others laugh is such a gift. As I've said, I'm not really a funny person, but I do love to laugh. Therefore, I'm a great audience! I like to be happy. To me, happiness is a choice. It's not some event that I'm waiting for, not something that happens to me. It's a choice I make every day.

I realize there are people who live in dire circumstances where happiness is a difficult choice to make. Many people suffer from addictions, abuse, illness, and other things. I admire those who can still find some happiness and smile with bravery when their lives are difficult. I'm talking more about the normal, day in, day out, routine, or unremarkable day of life. Be happy with what you have. This is increasingly difficult living in a country where everyone is trying to sell you something. New and improved products, changing trends, you deserve more rhetoric. Suddenly, what you have doesn't look good enough. Choose to be happy with what you have. It's a dangerous trap to constantly look at what others have and never be satisfied.

Here's the part where I'm going to give you the secret to a happy life. It's one word. Are you ready? Here it is: *gratitude*. Recognize the blessings in your life, and be thankful for them. Be happy with what God has given you. That doesn't mean you can't have goals, dreams, and ambition, but be able to identify the goodness you already have before you, and be thankful for it.

Speaking of happiness, God wants us to be happy. (There *is* a lot of rejoicing in the Bible.) Our brain has four primary chemicals that can drive the positive emotions you feel throughout the day: dopamine, oxytocin, serotonin, and endorphins (happyfeed.com).

It states in part:

Oxytocin—chemical of comfort, like from a hug, friendship, trust, or love. (You get this from relationships with your family and friends.)

Dopamine—a chemical you feel when someone likes your

post on Instagram; it's short-lived. (Prayer will give you more positive thoughts producing dopamine, which makes you happier.)

Serotonin—chemical of pride, loyalty, or status. (This is released when you serve others.)

Endorphins—they are released in response to pain or from deep belly laughs. (Exercise, dance, or sing to help reduce stress.)

It is comforting to me knowing that God designed our brains for happiness. We all have those four chemicals provided for us right from the start. That being said, Mr. Mark E. Moore explains further in his book *Core 52* about other components of our happiness. Pay careful attention to "C."

A. Genetics—Some people are optimists or pessimists by nature. People have a different "set point" for happiness, but we all do have a natural propensity to happiness. Genetics accounts for about 50 percent of our happiness.

B. Circumstances—Mr. Moore explains how we spend much of our energy here to try to bring us happiness. The reality is that it actually only accounts for about *10 percent* of it. Furthermore, it is not long-lasting, an average of ninety days.

C. Choices—Your diet, rest, and relationships account for the remaining 40 percent of your happiness. You cannot control your genetics or really much of your circumstances; however, you can account for almost half of your happiness by ***making wise choices*** (Emphasis mine).

The Bible doesn't really talk about the brain at all. It does talk about the heart a lot. It also gives a lot of guidance for relationships, controlling your mind, and joy. Betterhelp.com says that God tells us to be happy more times in Scripture than any other command.

I can't explain why, but I get such a thrill when the science matches

God's design. This must be because it's a combination of the beautiful world God gave us and His Word. I get warm fuzzies thinking about how some of the food we eat strengthens the body part it resembles; how our bodies need eight hours of sleep, and that's how much darkness God gave us; how Jesus says he is the living water, breath of life, bread of life, and light of the world and science says we need water, air, food, and light to live; how God turns coal into diamonds, sand into pearls, and a worm into a butterfly and He gives us new life; and how our brains have four chemicals ready to help us be happy, which is His desire for us. The collision, or perhaps cohesion, of those kinds of events help me to visibly see God, and it coincides with how I feel about Him when I am studying His Word or singing praises. It unifies. It's miraculous. It's a visual reminder of His supremeness.

Jesus was a happy person. We often think of Him as a teacher, the one who suffered, the one who carries our burdens, the one who saved us. He did do all these things. We also need to remember that He was light sent to this world! I want you to think of Him with crowds of people following Him, embracing children, feeding the hungry, healing the sick, and turning water to wine at a wedding. Jesus liked to have fun! He had to! Otherwise, I don't think that many people would have followed Him. He was the life of the party.

Of course, there are stories in the Bible where He was angry, tired, hurting, tempted, and many other emotions. That's part of why He was here, so we know that He knows how we feel. I just want to be sure that you remember He was a cheerful man too. "And when He had said this, He showed them His hands and His feet. And while they still disbelieved for joy and were marveling, He said to them, 'Have you anything here to eat?'" (Luke 24:40-41) Jesus's response makes me smile.

I believe God has quite a sense of humor also. Simply looking at some of God's creations makes me laugh. Look up the blobfish, the star-nosed mole, the aye-aye, or the red-lipped batfish. They are comical creatures.

Another entertaining aspect of life is coincidences. I can't help but wonder how many times those are God's way of showing His sense of humor as well. A "Godwink" may be His divine intervention in a situation because He can intervene any way He chooses, even in a funny "coincidence."

Charlie Chaplin believed that the most lost day in life is the day we don't laugh. He was a British comedian who starred in many silent films beginning in the early 1900s. Yes, he was even before *my* time. Even though he appeared in silent films, he certainly had a lot of great quotes. Chaplin had a difficult life but "espoused his faith in both God and humanity," and he cautioned "we think too much and feel too little." (georgiabulletin.org) One reason I admire him so much is because he must've believed as I do, adoring the merging of Earth and the Almighty. He said:

"If you see the moon, you will see the beauty of God...If you see the sun, you will see the power of God...If you see a mirror, you will see God's best creation. So believe in yourself..."

Life is so good! God has given us so many wonderful gifts here to enjoy. We have a beautiful earth, wonderful people, and a God who loves us. Sure, we all have bad days, but life is still marvelous! Smile and laugh every day. Thank God every day for the blessings He has given you. Choose happiness.

"If you feel stressed, give yourself a break and enjoy some ice cream, chocolates, candy, cake. Why? Because stressed spelled backwards is desserts."

—Charlie Chaplin

• • • Chapter 8 Questions • • •

1. Are you happy?
2. How do you picture Jesus?
3. What makes you laugh?
4. Tell a joke...
5. What are you grateful for?
6. Identify a time when you chose to be happy.

I know that there is nothing better for people
than to be happy and do good while they live.

1 Ecclesiastes 3:12 niv

CHAPTER 9

The Bible

The Bible is the best-selling book of all time. It is the foundation of Christianity. It is a gift from God. It is a gift of love. The Bible is our guide book on how we are to live on this Earth. It will teach you about love, life, death, how to treat others, how to worship God, relationships, money, right vs. wrong, happiness, suffering, all kinds of emotions, and forgiveness, to name a few. It will teach you about who He is. It is His Word. It is God Himself. It is very important for you to know that it is a book that has been proven to be historical text. That means it is not opinion, but is considered to be accurate. It is true.

Even though it was written so long ago, and yes, even though it is really, really old, the sins and life lessons are the same as those we experience today. We like to think we've come so far, and we have in many ways: the progress we've made to make our lives easier, our man-made environment, and our daily routines in life are vastly different. But inside, mankind is *not* different. The sins in the Bible are the sins we continue to do every day. Therefore, the Bible's teachings very much apply to us now.

I hold the Bible in very high esteem, but I am no Bible scholar. I'm simply sharing with you some of the basics. One of my regrets in life is that I cannot quote much scripture. It's embarrassing to admit. I believe God's Word, and I know quite well what it says to do. I try very hard to live what it says, but I wish I could speak directly from it and not have to paraphrase. I guess you could say I (try to) walk the walk, but I can't talk the talk. God wants me to do both. That's one I'm going to have to answer for. "But he answered, 'It is written, Man shall not live by bread alone, but by every word that comes from the mouth of God.'" (Matthew 4:4) Start learning scripture while you're young. Then don't stop.

"Because the Bible says so" is not the only reason why we are Christians. We are Christians because Jesus was born, said he would die at our hands and arise from the dead in three days, and He did! That is why we put our faith in Jesus. The act of Jesus coming, dying, and returning as He said He would is the reason we believe what the Bible says. The Bible is the resource we use. Don't become a Christian only because the Bible says to. Become a Christian because you believe Jesus was born of The Virgin Mary, died for your sins, was resurrected, and lives in Heaven seated at the right hand of God the Father. He is still here with us on this Earth through the Holy Spirit.

Where to Begin

When you begin reading the Bible, I suggest you start in the New Testament. It's easier reading. Joining a youth group would be helpful to begin your study. My hope and prayer is that when you read it, it speaks to your heart.

Big Insights by Marshall Coleman explains how "the Bible itself naturally divides believers into Jewish (Old Testament) and Christian (New Testament). Many of the Jews rejected Jesus and his message, so Paul brought his message to the Gentiles (that's most of us), and they became known as Christians."

The Old Testament takes place before Jesus. The New Testament takes place during and after Jesus's life. In the Old Testament, you could not have a personal relationship with God. You had to go through the chosen priests or prophets, who served as mediators between God and mankind. You can research the tearing of the Temple's Veil (Curtain) at the time of Jesus's death. God literally tore the massive veil in half from the top down at Jesus's last breath. It symbolized there would be no more separation between us and God. Before Jesus, you had to sacrifice animals to reconcile with God for your sins. Christianity.com says that "God required animal sacrifices as a way for His people to temporarily atone for their sins and draw nearer to Him. Ultimately, the sacrifices pointed to the severity of sin and the coming ultimate sacrificial death, that of Jesus Christ."

Man had a difficult time following all the rules in the Old Testament. So, God sent His son here as He said He would. Jesus came and showed us how to live. He was perfect. Yet He took on our sins, making Himself the sin so we could be righteous. We traded. What a gift! His blood shed for us as He died on the cross meant that we no longer had to offer blood sacrifices.

Jesus made it possible for us to have a personal relationship with God. The Holy Spirit came so that God can be with *each* of us. We no longer needed a prophet to intercede. This gives us personal access to God all by ourselves, if we make that choice. This is very powerful. *We have personal access to everything God is.* That statement is breathtaking! Do not underestimate the potential of that statement in your life.

What are the Odds?

In the Old Testament, there were many references to the Messiah coming. In *Core 52* (again), Mark E. Moore says there are seven prophecies that tell about the Messiah. They are specific and unexpected, he says, which makes them substantial in their vision. The probability of these passages being fulfilled by one man is only 1 in 100,000,000,000,000,000—that's one in one hundred quadrillion. Mr. Moore explains there are also another fifty major prophecies about Jesus's life and death, and dozens of minor references. This staggering statistic is impossible to ignore and foolish to reject—especially when eternity is at stake. Don't let this be the thing where you decide to play the odds.

The Bible was written by forty different people. If you think about *two* people growing up on the same street, in the same socioeconomic class, and ask them their opinions on religion, love, emotions, family, morals, sin, relationships, and all the other areas of life, there's a legitimate chance their opinions will be very different, or at least vary in some aspects. But the Bible's forty authors of various backgrounds and time periods have the same message in these areas. The message from God is real.

Many have studied the Bible to try to discredit it but with no luck. All of these authors were spoken to by God. *Remember, the Bible has been proven to be a reputable source of history.* That's why it has been around for so long and will continue to be.

I admit that when you're reading the Bible, sometimes it is confusing. It may be hard to relate to because of the language or ancient way of life. It's important to understand the Bible in context, to know what was happening at the particular time it was written. There are many good resources that explain the events of the Bible in their historical context. That's why you should find a church where a preacher explains God's Word in a way that is interesting to you and speaks to your heart. That's why you should join a Bible Study or youth group so you can focus on certain topics of the Bible and learn from the other people in your group. That's why you should choose Christian friends, so you can share what you've learned and how God works in your lives. I have learned from so many people!

When you're looking for answers from God, I don't recommend that you just open up the Bible, close your eyes, point to a verse, and go with that as your answer. That may not be the way He wants to answer you. That is putting God on the spot. God has many ways to communicate with you (See Ch. 13). Many Bibles have a concordance in the back that can be used to look up a specific need you may have. It will tell you where to look in the Bible for that precise guidance.

SOMETIMES THE BIBLE IS CONFUSING

There are some interesting things about the Bible I've learned along the way that I think could be easily misconstrued. For instance, you can find in the Bible, "An eye for any eye, and a tooth for a tooth." This might lead you to believe that if someone hits you, you should hit him back! The Bible also says, "But I tell you, do not resist an evil person. If anyone slaps you on the right cheek, turn to them the other cheek also. And if anyone wants to sue you and take your shirt, hand over your coat as well." That makes it confusing. What are you suppose to do? Slap them? Or turn the other cheek?

In the Old Testament, when God was giving us laws to live by, "an eye for an eye" referred to justice under the law: He wanted us to be sure that the punishment fit the crime. Don't make the punishment more harsh than is needed; yet make sure it is harsh enough to serve its purpose. This came to be abused, so when Jesus came (New Testament), he said that in our daily living we are to turn the other cheek. We are to be kind and love everyone, even those who you feel may not deserve it.

Another confusing Bible verse you may come across is: "Delight yourself in the Lord and He will give you the desires of your heart." (Psalm 37:4) It makes it sound like, if you love God, He'll give you whatever you want. However, it means that when you love the Lord, your heart will be changed, and you will desire what is right because He will be in your heart. As a Christian, we are not supposed to want selfish things. When you become a Christian, hopefully, you will want the right things. Your purpose will become putting others first. When you read the Bible, I think it can be easy to misconstrue some verses. That is why it's important to study His Word.

Don't be under the illusion that once you're a Christian all your troubles will be solved. Christians have the same troubles as everyone else. The difference is, when you put God in control and pray about it, He will work His good in the situation. Something good will come out of it. You will know that whatever happens, He thinks that is best. As much as we love our fathers on Earth, He is so much more. You can trust in Him completely.

Here's another confusing concept I've heard in sermons or conversations: Sin is sin. It makes it sound like all sin is the same. God hates all sin, no matter what the sin is. But I do not believe that all sin is equal. If I told Mrs. Mabel that her peach pie was delicious when in truth it was a little dry, is that the same as Mr. Pedophile who rapes children? There is no way the just God we serve sees those as the same. What is true is that everyone is a sinner. Do not think you will stand before God and say, "Well, I wasn't as bad as so-and-so!" The point is, you are still a sinner. You will have to stand there and answer for your sins, no matter what they are. So "sin is sin" means we all have it. All sin is bad. No one is perfect. Some sins are more serious than others. Biblically, one example of this would be in Luke 12:47-48. Two slaves are judged by the returning master according to what they each knew, even though they each did what was wrong (biola.edu). Another example is when Jesus explained that evil thoughts are still sin, even if you don't act on it. (Matthew 5:21-28) But that doesn't mean that thinking about murder and committing murder are *equal* sins. However, both are sins.

Furthermore, if all sin was equal, why would we have to be judged? We'd all have the same fate. I believe the number of sins or kinds of sins you commit matter very much. As a Christian, though, you can be forgiven, no matter what the sin is, if you ask. As a non-Christian, your sins are not forgiven, so they will determine your eternity.

Also, there are parts of the Bible that may sound a little crazy. It does not lack for exciting, astonishing stories. However, when you're a Christian, you must embrace all of the Bible. Once you start picking and choosing the parts you want to believe, the foundation crumbles. If you believe in God, then you must believe His Word. All of it.

Finally, there are two common words you'll hear in Christianity. They are mercy and grace. They are not the same thing. **Grace** is when God gives us what we don't deserve. **Mercy** is when God spares us from what we do deserve. (**Blessings** are when He is generous with both.)

Kinda Sorta Biblical

There are also popular sayings or quotes you'll come across that people think came from the Bible, yet they did not. Here are some that are kinda-sorta biblical or not at all biblical.

- *Cleanliness is next to godliness.* This saying is not meant to be taken literally, at least from the Bible's standpoint. When you pray for forgiveness of your sins, you are cleansing your heart, which will draw you closer to God. The Bible says in James 4:8: "Draw near to God and He will draw near to you. Cleanse your hands, you sinners; and purify your hearts, you double-minded."
- *All things work together for good.* Romans 8:28 reads in full: "And we know that in all things God works for the good *of those who love Him*, who have been called according to His purpose." (Emphasis is mine.) Therefore, if you are not a Christian, all things will not necessarily work together for good. You'll be rolling the dice.
- *Money is the root of all evil.* The Bible says in 1 Timothy 6:10: "For the love of money is a root of all kinds of evil. Some people, eager for money, have wandered from the faith and pierced themselves with many griefs." This means that the *love* of money is evil, not money itself.
- *God moves in mysterious ways.* We believe that is true; however, in the Bible it is stated as: "For my thoughts are not your

thoughts, neither are your ways my ways, declares the LORD."
(Isaiah 55:8)

- *God helps those who help themselves.* This is definitely not true.
  God does some of His best work on those who are helpless. It
  may be how He shows you that He is in control and there is
  nothing He can't do. If you can't help yourself, just ask God for
  help. He will be there. Self-help is not a requirement. You don't
  need anything but the desire to know Him.

- *To thine own self be true.* This is from Shakespeare's *Hamlet.* The
  Bible says the opposite. We are to constantly put others before
  ourselves. This is a consistent theme in the Bible. We are to
  serve others. Treat your neighbor as yourself.

- *The Seven Deadly Sins—Gluttony, Greed, Sloth, Lust, Vanity,
  Envy, Wrath.* These are never grouped together in the Bible,
  but they are hated by the Lord. Proverbs 6:16-19 states: "These
  six things the LORD hates, seven that are detestable to Him:
  haughty eyes, a lying tongue, hands that shed innocent blood,
  a heart that devises wicked schemes, feet that are quick to rush
  into evil, a false witness who pours out lies and a person who
  stirs up conflict in the community." If you have committed any
  one or more of these sins, you can always receive salvation once
  you repent and believe.

There are many more misconceptions. Hopefully, you get the idea
that it is important to know what the Bible says. Just because something
sounds biblical doesn't mean that it's true. And it is very easy for messages
to be misinterpreted.

I am not worried about your choice of vocation. I am sure you will be
successful in your life, if you want to be, whatever you choose to do. I have
faith in you because I know your parents. I am more worried about you
knowing God. Simply learning what is in the Bible is not enough. Satan
knows what is in the Bible. I know I'm supposed to exercise thirty minutes

every day. Knowing I'm suppose to do that doesn't make me healthy. I have to actually do it. The same goes for the Bible. Knowing what is in it isn't really going to help you unless you actually love God. Use the Bible to guide you, but absolutely pursue a relationship with Him. Love God and serve others. How well you do these two things will determine your eternity. That's His plan.

> "Blessed is the one who reads aloud the words of this prophecy, and blessed are those who hear it and take to heart what is written in it."

> Revelation 1:3

• • • CHAPTER 9 QUESTIONS • • •

1. Can you quote scripture?

2. Weigh the value of this statement: *We have personal access to everything God is.*

3. Do you think the Bible is too old?

4. How have you experienced God's grace? His mercy? What about His blessings?

5. Do you have any questions about something in the Bible you think is confusing?

6. Examine the probability of Jesus fulfilling prophesies.

The entirety of Your word is truth, and
every one of Your righteous judgments
endures forever.

PSALM 119:160 NKJV

CHAPTER 10

Prayer

I want to tell you how I have come to believe this great big Earth has been set up. Clearly, I have no proof, but this is what helps me make sense of this splendid world that also has so much evil in it. I believe that prayer is so important.

GOD IS THE CLOCKMAKER

I believe God made everything, like he said in Genesis. He was the clock-maker who started off time. This Earth was designed, and everything God made was very good. (Genesis 1:31) Sometimes it seems as though He gives us glimpses of Heaven on Earth. Oh, the beauty! Then, after the fall of man (Adam and Eve eating the apple from the Tree of Life), sin was introduced to us. So now we have glimpses of Hell on Earth too. The decisions you make while you live here will determine where you will spend eternity—Heaven or Hell. During your brief time here, if you choose to follow God's rules, asking for forgiveness when you don't, and love Him by loving your fellow man, you'll spend eternity in Heaven. If you choose not to follow Him, you won't go to Heaven.

Now, as the clockmaker, God can see everything He designed and how it is operating. Earth will operate within all the scientific and mathematical laws that God designed, including the Law of Probability. Expressed mathematically, probability is the number of ways a specified event can occur, divided by the total number of all possible event occurrences (sciencing.com). Chances are, sometimes good things will happen to you, and sometimes bad things will happen to you. Obviously.

Let me clarify that I'm not talking about death here. Death is an inevitable bad thing that everyone will face eventually. No probability about it. It's a certainty. (Death is sad, because we'll miss being here with our loved ones, and then there's that fear of the unknown. But for Christians it's not a bad thing.)

I'm talking here about all of life's little events along the way. I understand why good things sometimes happen to bad people or bad things happen to good people. It's all in the Law of Probability. Sometimes things just happen.

However, I believe that if you pray about anything, the clockmaker will determine what is best for you or the situation and will react accordingly. Prayer is important for communicating with Him. Then if (or I should say *when*) you're dealing with something bad, it is comforting to know that at least He is in charge and knows what is best for reasons we may or may not understand. God will make something good come out of the situation if you are living with His Spirit.

Life Without Prayer Is Like Rolling the Dice

If you don't pray, it's like rolling the dice. The situation may turn out just fine. Or, it may not, and nothing good may come from it. It's a chance you're taking. I'm telling you, if you pray, the results you get will be comforting to you because first of all, you'll know that God is in control. The result is in His hands. Second of all, with His hand in it, it gives me so much peace of mind! No matter what I'm praying about, I know that the result is what He says is best. I can live with that. That is comfort. He is a God of knowledge and truth.

Rick Warren has said that sometimes life is like driving along and coming to a sharp curve in the road. You don't know what is around the curve, but God does. He is like a pilot above you and can see everywhere. He knows what is ahead for you. He knows what is best.

I have also heard tough times compared to an animal getting its paw caught in a trap. You have to apply pressure on the trap to release it, which initially causes more pain to the animal. It's hard for us to understand why we have to experience more pain, but it is inevitably for a reason. God will let us experience that pain knowing He's going to somehow make it better afterwards.

It's only a matter of time until life will hand you a difficult situation. In fact, that's when many people call for God. That's not the only time God wants to help you. He wants to have a relationship with you every day. "However, as it is written: 'What no eye has seen what no ear has heard, and what no human mind has conceived, the things God has prepared for those who love him.'" (1 Corinthians 2:9) If you don't have that relationship with Him, you're going to have to deal with all the hard times by yourself. Maybe a friend or family will help you, but they are not all-knowing. They don't even compare. They are just taking their best guess. Will that be what's best? Who knows! It's a roll of the dice.

Don't just roll the dice in life. That is doing life the hard way. I want you to lead a life where God blesses you in ways beyond your comprehension.

MY UNANSWERED PRAYER

During each of my three pregnancies, I always prayed for my babies to be healthy. The first two were. When I went through the motions and prayed that same prayer for the third time, totally expecting the same outcome, I was surprised when God decided not to "grant" my request. He decided to let our son be born with hypoplastic left heart syndrome (HLHS); his heart had a faulty valve and was a little small on the left side. This brought a halt to my life, which had been pretty awesome to that point. I couldn't help but wonder why God didn't answer my prayer.

"Why? Why? Why did you let this happen? Was my prayer not compassionate enough? Was I not persistent enough? Was it too routine?" I had a decision to make. I could've decided to be angry at God, or rely on Him to get through it all. I never really had to make a conscious decision. I was hurting so bad, I needed Him. There was no way I could do it without Him. I truly do not know how people get through those hard times in life without God. It must be so difficult. In the end, it drew me closer to Him. Is that part of the reason why it happened? I don't know. You don't always get your answers. You just have to have faith. God is more interested in your holiness than your happiness, not that He doesn't care about your happiness. I would've been happier if my son didn't have to go through any of it, but one good thing that did came from it is I became a stronger Christian through it all.

We watched our son go through a lot of pain and suffering his first eighteen months of his life. There's something God certainly knows about: watching your son suffer. His son suffered a lot more than mine did but for entirely different reasons.

Our son had three open-heart surgeries before he was two years old. He almost died after the first because of kidney failure, and again after the third because of an infection in his breastbone. Watching him go through all these surgeries, his small chest cut open three times, was very difficult. However, that suffering was necessary for the wonderful surgeons, doctors, nurses, and others to help him recover and heal. (Medical people: Talk about serving others—you take it to a whole new level! Thank you for what you do.) They helped him fight to live. His suffering was for his best interests. While it may have been difficult to watch our baby go through so much, it was to help him survive.

Jesus's suffering was not because of any kind souls trying to help him. Many hated him and wanted to watch him suffer. There's no way my son's suffering compares to His. Jesus suffered and carried the burden of your and my sins amidst those who were crucifying Him. He became our sin, so we could be made free of sin. The blood he shed was for all of us. Christians believe that Jesus's suffering is why we can be cleansed so God will forgive all our sins even though we are unworthy. God sent His son here to be crucified and die for all of us. That is God's love for you and me.

I remember praying a prayer during one of the many procedures my son had, watching him look at me helplessly with his face all scrunched up and beet red while tears rolled down his face because he couldn't cry out loud with the ventilator in his mouth. Tubes were coming out of him for fluid drainage and needles going into him for drugs to be administered. That image is forever ingrained in my mind. His eyes were pleading with me to do something, and I felt so helpless. As difficult as it was, I prayed for God to stop his suffering, however that may be.

We have two friends that also went through some severe medical treatments. Both survived and became Christians through their experiences. One was Eric, who had brain cancer. The other is our friend Chris, who had a terrible motorcycle accident and spent over a year recuperating. These life-altering experiences brought them to God. I do not believe God caused their pain, but He used the experiences to draw them nearer to Him. I am so glad that they came to walk in a closer relationship with God. It is quite a testament to God because now that they know His love, they're so happy to have discovered it, no matter how they got there. (Think about that: They are happy to have gone through cancer and a motorcycle accident, and are thankful for it. People who have not experienced God's love do not understand this.) God has such love for us, it would hurt Him to hurt us. God is love.

Hopes and Dreams

You will also have hopes and dreams. I'm sure you've already begun to think about your future somewhat. There is nothing wrong with working hard and having lofty dreams. We expect to work hard to achieve our dreams. That's a given. Give it all you got and have fun too! I am sure you will be successful if you have that desire.

We hope and dream that we'll get what we want. Even with hard work, there's no guarantee you'll end up where you are meant to be if you're doing it on your own. It's keeping your fingers crossed and rolling the dice. Prayer is whispering to God and telling Him your desires, then letting Him take control and participate in the outcome. Your success will have more meaning and purpose when God has led you where He wants you to be. He is just waiting to bless you. He wants to give you even more than what you ask. "Be strong and courageous. Do not be afraid or terrified because of them, for the Lord your God goes with you; he will never leave you nor forsake you." (Deuteronomy 31:6)

In the Bible, Jesus healed so many people. People longed to see Him, to be touched and healed by Him; even when they simply touched His robe, they were healed. Every time He was confronted with the death of a loved one, He brought them back to life (Lazarus, a little girl, and the son of a widow). I think this proves to us that Jesus understands our hurts. He showed compassion. We know that He knows how it feels to experience loss and hurt. He feels for us. He died for us because He loves us and wants to carry our sins.

I can picture God handing out our gifts like Oprah handing out cars: You get a beautiful singing voice! You get the ability to listen to others! And you—you get the kindest heart of compassion! And so on. However, I can't picture God saying, cancer for you! A motorcycle accident for you! You get a faulty heart! I believe all these things are possible because of man's fall into sin; therefore, there's evil in our world. But that's not how

God wants to treat us. He hurts when we hurt. But He will take that evil or hurt and use it for good.

Think of Him as your father. (He is!) I mean like your earthly father or mother. Most parents do not want to cause their children harm. The difference is, God has the power to do what is best. In each situation, I think God will play a role however He decides. Some of us get a second chance from accidents and illnesses, and some of us do not, for reasons only He knows.

Think of how your earthly father disciplines you. He does it because he loves you. I will not argue with God's ways. I respect His authority.

How to Pray

Prayer doesn't have to be difficult at first. You want it to be heartfelt to be effective. Personally, I'm not a real chatty person. I'm more of an internal thinker. I think about what I should have said about two days later. Just because I don't express verbally every thought going on in my brain doesn't mean I don't feel deeply. Prayer doesn't have to be wordy and "churchy." However, it is a skill you want to learn and improve upon. As long as it's sincere and from your heart, it will be compelling to Him. Here are two effective forms of prayer that may benefit you. The first is one I use in my everyday prayer.

Five-Finger Prayer here

1. Thumb—It's closest to your heart, so pray for those closest to you—your family and friends.
2. Pointer Finger—It's used to give directions. Pray for teachers, coaches, therapists, doctors, and first responders.
3. Middle Finger—It's the tallest. Pray for leaders in government, business, and the church.
4. Ring Finger—It's the weakest. Pray for the sick, poor, and those most in need.

5. Pinkie Finger—It's the smallest. Pray for yourself and your own needs.

This next one I wish I'd known of earlier. It would've been beneficial to use during my roughest seasons of life. Rick Warren tells us how to pray using the acronym CARE. He cites many examples of this method being used in the Bible. Use this prayer when you're hurting.

Complain: "Why, God?"
Tell God what you think is unfair, painful, etc. Complain in faith, and complain *to* God, not *about* God.

Appeal to God's nature.
"God, you know…" "I know who you are. You are powerful, loving, all knowing…"

Remind God of His promises.
Just like when we were children reminding our parents, "You promised!"

Express trust.
"I trust you God, even when I don't understand."

It's also definitely worth mentioning the prayer Jesus taught us to pray. Jesus said we should pray like this, shown in Matthew 6:9-13 and Luke 11:2-4:

Our Father who art in Heaven,
Hallowed [holy] be your name. Thy kingdom come.
Thy will be done,
on Earth as it is in Heaven.
Give us this day our daily bread.
And forgive us our trespasses [sins]   As we forgive those who
trespass against us.
And lead us not into temptation,
But deliver us from evil.

For thine is the kingdom, and the power, and the glory for
ever and ever.
Amen.

Music can also be used as prayer. Many Christian songs are quoting scripture. The book of Psalms is songs and prayers! Again, often I feel closest to Him when I'm singing Christian music. The words I'm singing reflect how I feel, and I never would have been clever enough to say those words myself. Prayerandpossibilities.com says music brings more meaning to scripture and prayer and is linked to memory and emotion. Music often speaks what our minds cannot. Songs work their way into our souls and help us express what's on our hearts. Music itself can be a form of prayer as we pray the lyrics or use the music to help us focus our hearts on God.

I started praying to God more fervently as I walked closer with Him. The most recent example of me truly relying on prayer to make a major decision in my life was at my retirement. At age fifty-one I retired from teaching, which is fairly young by most standards. I was young enough to think about what I might pursue next. Rusty and I thought it might be fun to open a Chick-Fil-A in our town. We thought, it's a Christian company. I could work and hopefully influence older children, be in the public eye in a different capacity than teaching, contribute more to our community, and give more financially. So I applied, and I prayed. I completely left it all up to God and did not fret about it once. I was perfectly content to leave it in His hands. If God wanted it to happen, it would happen. As it turned out, He did not want it to happen, and I was fine with His decision. I didn't understand why because I thought I could do so much, but I was still okay with it. I now know that He knew it was for the best.

Looking back, if I had started a new business I would not have been available for my mother-in-law after her stroke, for my dad during his cancer treatments and surgery, or for my aunt with Alzheimer's. God even gave me that first year of retirement to rest before all the sickness that was about to unfold. I am so grateful for the extra time I had with my loved ones. Also, I would've been so busy, I most likely never would've had time to come up with the idea to write this book. God had other plans for me in my retirement. His timing is so perfect. I trust Him completely.

LISTENING TO GOD

Pray to God about everything. God does speak to you, so make sure you are listening. Make sure you are paying attention. Focus. How many times do we say the words, again and again, expecting an answer to fall out of the sky, expecting God to resolve the situation right now? We want God to make it go away. Just fix it.

After you pray, you have to look for His answers. Be prepared to find an answer you hadn't considered. "For God does speak—now one way, now another—though no one perceives it." (Job 33:14) Sometimes we may not get an answer right away.

Why should we keep praying when there's no answer? Rick Warren reminds us that:

1. Persistent prayer focuses your attention. It's to remind YOU that God is the source of our needs.
2. Persistent prayer helps you clarify what you want. It separates deep longings from mere whims.
3. Persistent prayer tests your faith, which is the only way you can grow.
4. Persistent prayer prepares your heart for the answer you will receive. It helps you grow and get ready for a bigger and better answer.

Rather than think of God as "up there somewhere," remember He is right there beside you even if you aren't actually pursuing Him. He's waiting for you to acknowledge Him, talk to Him, ask Him for help. He's waiting for you to start that relationship. I like to imagine that Jesus is right there waiting to be a part of every aspect of my life.

Then, the Bible says Satan is like a lion that prowls around me and throws things at me, just waiting for a weak moment to tempt me or tell me I'm not good enough. "Be alert and of sober mind. Your enemy, the devil, prowls around like a roaring lion looking for someone to devour." (1 Peter 5:8) Satan is not always with you. Only God is that faithful. Only God knows your every thought and never leaves you. Satan can only see and hear you. He knows your weaknesses from what he has seen or heard, therefore influencing your thoughts or tempting your actions. Nowhere in the Bible does it say that Satan knows your thoughts. He is not all-knowing or all-powerful like God. Vocalizing Bible verses or singing praises will help you defeat evil thoughts. Satan hates that. "Put on the full armor of God, so that you can take your stand against the devil's schemes." Ephesians 6:11

I am constantly steering my thoughts toward God, not just in times of trouble, but in my day-to-day living. I'm not sure if it's because I'm retired now and have more time, because I'm walking closer with Him now, or because of this mission I'm on to write to you. Our minds easily drift, so I want my thoughts to be positive and directed.

Back in my day, cartoons often portrayed people with a dilemma as having a little angel sitting on one shoulder and a devil sitting on the other, each trying to persuade the person to behave a certain way. I wonder if they may not be too far off track! Both are there, watching to see what choice you make. Both are vying for your attention. The choice is yours. I'm sure it's more sophisticated than that, but I'm a visual learner, so I can relate to those childhood images.

The devil doesn't only tempt us on the big choices between good and evil. Given a choice between obvious good and evil, most of us would choose good. Most people don't *blatantly* lie, cheat, or steal from our fellow man. No, we're much more subtle. So is Satan. When I think of The Ten Commandments, there are a couple that I can handle upholding very easily: Thou shall not kill. Check. Honor thy father and mother.

No problem. Thou shall not take the Lord God's name in vain. Never! Adultery? No thank you.

The other six commandments get a little murky for me. Satan doesn't waste his time with me on those four, but I am sure there is some version of the rest that I have dabbled in. He's sly enough to prey on my weaknesses in subtle ways: You're not good enough; you can't write a book. Putting snacks in your bag when you go to the movies isn't really stealing; you buy their popcorn. Admiring the physique of professional football players isn't lust; it's admiring God's handiwork! Doing chores on Sunday isn't unholy; you went to church. And the list goes on. Yes, he is very tricky. Subtlety is his specialty.

Prayer Changes You

Scientific research shows that prayer works. There are *many* studies that show the significance of praying and health outcomes. They are so numerous that there are now one hundred and one medical schools that incorporate patient spirituality in their curriculum ("The power of prayer: Science proves it works, has positive psychological effects" foxnews.com).

I set aside time daily to spend in God's Word. I also pray throughout the day as people enter my mind or as I check my prayer list. Often, I just talk to God. When you talk to Him throughout the day, it gives Him the opportunity to live in this world through your eyes. He loves to participate in your life rather than wait idly by to be acknowledged. We are told to take everything to God in prayer. "Do not be anxious about anything, but in every situation, by prayer and petition, with thanksgiving, present your requests to God." (Philippians 4:6) The big stuff and the little stuff.

I have the most difficult time praying when someone has hurt me or someone I love. I don't want to pray for them because in the moment, I'm perfectly content with them *not* knowing God so they can spend eternity burning in Hell! Isn't that awful?! I am embarrassed to even tell you that. It hasn't happened very many times, but still, that is an ugly feeling.

I allow myself a couple of days, maybe weeks—okay, on a couple occasions it's been months—to fume, and then I start to pray for the little culprit. Praying for someone who has hurt you is very difficult at first. But I promise you, your heart begins to change. You will gradually release the resentment you have harbored in your heart. In the long run, you will benefit physically as well as emotionally when you free yourself of the maliciousness. Praying for your enemies, as crazy as that sounds, will be therapeutic for you, and it is one of the most Christian acts you can do.

However, do not do it just for the benefits you receive from it. Do it because we are called to love our enemies. "But I tell you, love your enemies and pray for those who persecute you." (Matthew 5:44) As Christians, we are to love everyone. It's easy to love the people you like. It's a challenge to love the people you don't like. But others will see God's love in you when you set this example. It ain't easy! Trust me; it will change your heart.

When you go through hard times, it is best to ask for God's guidance during your trials so you know how to respond, and it's always crucial for you to reflect on what role you played in the situation. I wonder how many times people have had to pray for me because of hurt I've caused them? Sometimes it's hard to reflect amidst the hurt, but there's always a good chance that your attitude may need some adjusting. Rarely is it completely the other person's fault. Check in with God always. Read your Bible.

I'll end on the lighter side with a joke about prayer. It's an oldie but a goodie:

So far today, God, I've done all right. I haven't gossiped, haven't lost my temper, haven't been greedy, grumpy, nasty, selfish, or over-indulgent. I'm really glad about that.

But in a few minutes, God, I'm going to get out of bed and from then on I'm probably going to need a lot more help.

• • • Chapter 10 Questions • • •

1. Have you prayed persistently for something?
2. What is your dream?
3. What pain have you experienced?
4. How do you pray? Do your prayers differ?
5. When do you pray?
6. Have you ever left something completely in God's hands?
7. How do you picture God, Jesus, and the Holy Spirit?
8. What subtle ways does Satan tempt you?
9. Have you ever prayed for an enemy?
10. Analyze your role in a drama situation.
11. Is there an area in your life where you're rolling the dice?
12. Cite a medical example of how prayer helped heal.

Devote yourselves to prayer with an alert
mind and a thankful heart.

Colossians 4:2 nlt

CHAPTER 11

Life After Life

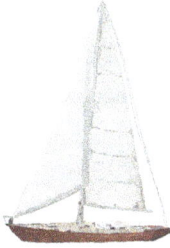

Death is not the end; your soul continues.

Melancholy subject. Death is an enigma to me, as it is to most people. I asked God a long time ago to let me die at a time when He can make the most use of it. Please use me the best way You can so others may know You. I am completely confident in the timing of my death being in His hands. I don't think I'm scared to die. I'm not looking forward to the process of dying. Not knowing exactly everything is a little intimidating. However, I know my afterlife will be glorious. I admit, I get excited when I think about how wonderful it will be. I am not anxious to die, though. Mainly because it makes me sad when I think about who may not be there. I'm going to miss some people.

JUDGMENT

I've pondered a lot about death and the afterlife. For example, once you die, how will you be judged? This worries me. The thought of standing before Him and having to justify some of my choices will not be pleasant. I have some reprieve from my angst! I recently was reminded that Christians will be judged differently from non-Christians.

We Christians take communion and ask for forgiveness of our sins, which is given. All our sins are forgotten. That is possible because of the sacrifice Jesus made for us. Therefore, we Christians will not be judged for our sins because they have been wiped clean. Whew! Thank you, Jesus! However, we will be judged for our actions, such as: Did you use the gifts God gave you? How did you act toward your fellow man? Did you try to teach others about Jesus? Did you love and serve God and others? God knows your heart. You can't keep secrets from Him. He is the only one who knows your every thought. Your heart will determine your eternity. This is the heart of Christianity.

If you are *not* a Christian, you have not asked for forgiveness of your sins; therefore, when you die you will be judged for all of your sins *and* your actions. You will have to answer for them both. Be afraid.

Heaven

I wonder: Is Heaven one big place? There are some verses that elude to different levels of Heaven, one being, "So the last will be first, and the first will be last." (Matthew 20:16) This refers to a definite order. It gives me comfort when I see someone born with severe physical/mental disadvantages. Some people are born into such difficult lives. It warms my heart knowing that they may have a glorious eternity. God is so just. They deserve a peaceful eternity.

Another verse states, "My Father's house has many rooms; if that were not so, would I have told you that I am going there to prepare a place for you?" (John 14:2) So, He is preparing a special place for each of us (Christians). Does it stand to reason some places may be better than others? Or, does that simply mean it will be a big place?

Also, you will be rewarded for your works. This is not to be confused with a belief that your works will get you into Heaven. They absolutely will not, but you will be rewarded for good works once you've made it there. This also makes me think that maybe there are different levels. Ephesians 2:8-9, "For by grace you have been saved through faith. And this is not your own doing; it is the gift of God, not a result of works, so that no one may boast." And Matthew 6:1 states, "Watch out! Don't do your good deeds publicly, to be admired by others, for you will lose the reward from your Father in Heaven."

Surely, no one knows for sure how it all works. Again, God wants us to have faith in Him. No sense worrying about it (if you're a Christian). We have no control over how it's designed, although it's very interesting to ponder. The afterlife is one of those subjects with some ambiguity. Actually, the Bible gives a lot of descriptions of Heaven; it's simply difficult for us to understand or to even imagine. All I know is that it will be amazing! "For he was looking forward to the city with foundations, whose architect and builder is God." (Hebrews 11:10) When you think about how beautiful *this* place is, can you imagine how much greater Heaven will be? God is spending even more time preparing a place for us there. I wonder if God saved some special colors for us to see only in Heaven?

HEAVEN VS. THE MASSES

You may notice when you attend a funeral that many assume the soul is in Heaven. Why is that? That's easy, because it hurts too bad to envision the opposite. When I die, I hope the preacher infuses a little bit of fire and brimstone in my eulogy. This is when you have a captive audience with death on their minds. Preach it!

The Bible says that not many will make it to Heaven. "Enter by the narrow gate. For the gate is wide and the way is easy that leads to *destruction*, and those who enter by it are *many*. For the gate is narrow and the way is hard that leads to *life*, and those who find it are *few*." (Matthew 7:13-14) (Emphasis is mine.)

I saw a funny sign on a church marquis: *The fact that there's a "Highway to Hell" and only a "Stairway to Heaven" says a lot about anticipated traffic numbers.* (You may have to Google those song titles. Yes, they are songs from the 1970s, which is when I grew up. I would've been about your age now.) I say it's funny; I guess because I know those songs. The reality is, it is very sad. When I think of the billions of people who have lived on the Earth, I feel insignificant and therefore helpless when I'm told not many will be admitted to Heaven. We Christians keep plugging along, though! We are trying to win more souls. I'm just going to be honest here, though: It's very defeating to think that we live in a world where most people are not going to Heaven, yet we are supposed to love and serve them? Yes, that is exactly what God wants us to do. Win more souls. Never stop trying.

Now that you've heard about God, your defense when you die cannot be, "Well, I didn't know! No one ever told me about you." That is true for all non-Christians. If you've heard but didn't respond, "not knowing" cannot be your defense. That is also why missionaries are very important. I am so happy that people are dedicated to spreading God's Word. Please support missionaries.

Heaven's Requirements

So what do you have to do to get into Heaven? This part of the Bible is *very* clear. Here are the steps:

1. *Hear* God's Word and *believe* that Jesus is the Son of God.
2. Accept that you will not go to Heaven unless you become saved in Christ; *confess* your sins.
3. Ask Jesus to come into your heart through prayer and salvation; *repent* (feel sorry for your past actions).
4. *Be baptized* as a sign of your commitment to Christ, and pledge to follow Him the rest of your life.

What if you were baptized as an infant? There's no example of an infant baptism in the Bible. My church believes it has to be a choice that you make. Babies can be *dedicated* in a special service where their family promises to raise them in the church. This does not guarantee them a place in Heaven as an adult. But we do believe that children who die will go to Heaven. But Jesus said, "Let the little children come to me and do not hinder them, for to such belongs the kingdom of Heaven." (Matthew 19:13-14) This also makes my heart happy. Innocent children will be sent to Heaven because He is so loving, gracious, and just. It only seems fair, since children are so pure and have not had the life experiences to be exposed to God, all He has to offer, and the opportunity to make a choice by following the steps. *Jesus loves the little children.* A song ensues in my mind.

You may be wondering, "What are the age requirements to be considered a child?" The answer is, I don't know. Fevr.net says, "The age of accountability is the concept that those who die before reaching the age of accountability are automatically saved by God's grace and mercy. The age of accountability is the belief that God saves all those who die never having possessed the ability to make a decision for or against Christ."

You, and only you, are responsible for your salvation in the end. Then God will judge you.

I am so glad that I serve a righteous God. He knows all. That frees me from the burden of judging others. Let Him do it. We are called to love and serve others. Love and serve. That's it. That's hard enough some days. Do not add the extra burden of judging on top of it. You're giving yourself extra work. Release it to Him.

> "Do not judge, or you too will be judged. For in the same way
> you judge others, you will be judged, and with the same measure you use, it will be measured to you."
>
> Matthew 7:1-2

Please note that none of those four steps above say anything about being good or nice. Christians typically are good and nice. (If they are not, I would question how well they know God.) If you are good and nice but do not do any of those four steps, I believe you will *not* be going to Heaven. The Bible is clear what God expects us to do. Simply being good and nice are not enough to get you there.

What if you only do one of the steps above? Or two? Does that mean you won't go to Heaven? I've heard this explained with an analogy: There's a ship out at sea that needs to dock safely in a bay surrounded by massive, jagged rocks. I can tell you a path that will guarantee your safe arrival at port. You should take it. There are other paths you can take that may get you there safely, but there's only one *sure* path you can choose. You are the ship; the port is Heaven. So does it mean there's no other way to get to Heaven? No. You may make it safely on another path. But why would you risk it? The Bible tells us exactly what to do. Why wouldn't you take the safe path for something as serious as your eternity?

Don't Put Off Your Faith

I know why. And this is the thing that hinders many, many people. You want to live life your own way here on Earth. You know better. You will have more fun. Why waste my life serving others when I can have fun and be in control myself? You're thinking, I'll do that religious stuff when I'm older. While I'm young, I want to have fun.

I see several problems with living that way. First, young people die every day. Some die suddenly. You may not have the chance to do the religious thing. Life can be taken from you in an instant. It's that Law of Probability. Sadly, it happens a lot.

Second, older people get set in their ways. Guilty. I am not changing my religion or my politics at this stage of my life. I like what I like. I've had many years to form my opinions. My mind is not as open and flexible to new ideas as it used to be. I try to keep an open mind; it's just not easily changed. If you want to change my mind about where we're meeting for lunch, my mind is wide open! But the big stuff? Not likely.

My experience with teaching the elderly about God too has not been fruitful. Churches today spend much of their effort on young families, and rightfully so. It's not that we don't care about older unbelievers. We absolutely do! It's just that older people are not always open to new ways. They've had many, many years to establish their habits and belief systems.

Third, older people may not have the mental capacity to understand new concepts. The brain may be physically unable to change. Nia.nih. gov says as a person gets older, certain parts of the brain shrink, especially those important to learning and other complex mental activities.

Although, I do believe there are people on their deathbeds that cry out to God and will be forgiven and embraced by Him. People dying a slow death can also become Christians at the end of their lives if they reach out to Him. It doesn't matter what you've done here on Earth, God will accept you if you ask. God is forgiving. God is merciful. I believe he'll give you clear up to the very last second on Earth to accept Him because God "wants all men to be saved and to come to a knowledge of the truth." (1 Timothy 2:4)

Recently, an older friend, Damon, shared his faith story with me. When he was twenty-eight years old and worked in the coal mine, part of the mine collapsed on top of him, smothering him. He said he felt his last breath leave his body, so he called out to God. Instantly, peace came over him. Coworkers dug him out and he survived. From that moment on, he never had any desire to drink, smoke, or swear again. He has lived the rest of his life for God.

> "If you declare with your mouth, 'Jesus is Lord,' and believe in your heart that God raised him from the dead, you will be saved. For it is with your heart that you believe and are justified, and it is with your mouth that you profess your faith and are saved."
>
> Romans 10:9-10

I believe that God knows when you are going to die, and so he gives you right up until that very last second to call out to Him. That's how much He loves us. He wants so badly to have a relationship with you. "The Lord is not slow in keeping his promise, as some understand slowness. He is patient with you, not wanting anyone to perish, but everyone to come to repentance." (2 Peter 3:9) But you must decide that *while you're here*. Some of those who call out to Him may be chosen to stay here longer to be used to further God's kingdom, like my friend Damon. Some, God may decide to go ahead and bring on home to Him. This may bring some comfort to those who lost someone who may not have spent time here following God, but perhaps in those last moments reached out for Him just before their death.

It's important to remember, though: Once you're dead, that's it. There will be no excuses at your judgment. You must decide here while you're still living. What if He asks you, "Did you know me? Did you love me?" What will you say? "So then each of us shall give account of himself to God." (Romans 14:12)

So yes, I'm sure God accepts you even at the last minute. It's just not a method I would recommend. You never know if you'll really have that opportunity.

This is the last, but certainly not the least important reason not to put off your faith. This is one of my most treasured bits of information I can pass on to you. Pay attention! This is important. *If you wait until you're old to become a Christian, you will not have time to become the person God designed you to be. You may not have the time to fulfill your purpose.* This is a process that takes time. Believe me! I have grown so much since I first became a Christian. I still have a long way to go. When I go to Heaven, I'm already going to have to explain why I didn't use my God-given gifts for Him earlier or why I didn't serve others better while on Earth.

My father and father-in-law were great men. Many people loved them. We were fortunate to have their love and influence in our lives. Each was married to a strong Christian woman, which ultimately led each of them to Christ later in their lives. As great as those men were, I can only imagine how much greater they would've been if they were walking with the Lord sooner. I will never know.

Our family appears to be in this cycle of strong Christian women leading their families. Thank you, Lord, for them! The Christian family is so much stronger when it's led by both the mother and the father. The family unit will be more secure and solid. Please take this to heart.

If you think you'll do the Christian thing *someday*, later, you're rolling the dice again. It's a gamble. That's doing life the hard way. I do not think it is wise to gamble with eternity.

Angels

After I'm dead, you may think of me every once in awhile. That'd be nice. What I don't want you to do is think that I'm going to be watching over you. Sorry, I know that sounds cruel when it's such a sweet sentiment. I expect to be very happy in Heaven, and I expect Him to keep his promise to be with *you* always: "…and teaching them to obey everything I have commanded you. And surely I am with you always, to the very end of the age." (Matthew 28:20)

There are no tears in Heaven. "He will wipe every tear from their eyes. There will be no more death or mourning or crying or pain, for the old order of things has passed away." (Revelation 21:4) So, when I'm gone, I will not be able to experience sadness. And if I am watching over you, and you are hurting, that would make me cry. I want you to learn to call on God at all times, good and bad. He can help you. God loves you even more than I do. Who knows? Maybe I'll be able to peek in on you on one of your happy days.

I believe in angels too. I admit, it confuses me to think of them watching over me because if God is always with me, why would I need them? No offense, angels, but why order the chopped liver when you have steak in front of you?

Luckily, my daily devotional book, *Core 52*, explains what angels do. They are messengers, announcing Jesus whenever he comes; assistants to believers in carrying out their call; and they affirm those God approves, which means if you are in company with an angel, you're marked as a person of God's. Therefore, I believe that Christians have guardian angels!

I read a story a long, long time ago in one of those *Chicken Soup for the Soul* books. The police had caught a rapist and were looking to build their case, so they put out his picture and asked if anyone had seen him on a particular night in a particular neighborhood. A young woman responded saying that she had seen him then and there. After the man was convicted, the police were curious so they asked the rapist why he hadn't raped *this* particular young woman. He said he would have, but she was walking between two large men. The woman said she had been walking alone.

This does not mean that if you're a Christian, you will never be raped. It is so difficult to understand how or why some of us have to live through such vile experiences. The "Why me?" question surfaces a lot before God, I would guess. I've questioned it myself about my son's heart defect. In any regard, I believe that God had a purpose for this young woman. Perhaps the angels were there to be sure she was able to carry out her calling. She was provided with two angels to protect her so she could fulfill her purpose.

I think we would be surprised to see how angels (and demons) are working around us or beside us. They can come in human form to assist believers. There are examples in the Bible. I believe we have angels walking amongst us. "Do not forget to entertain strangers, for by so doing some people have entertained angels without knowing it." (Hebrews 13:2)

Hopefully, we will reunite—or unite, whichever the case may be—in Heaven. This reminds me of a sermon I heard a long time ago that *blew my mind.* If I'm in Heaven, and if one of my loved ones doesn't make it there, and if there are no tears in Heaven, then I must not have a memory of those loved ones. Whoa! Since God is our creator, He can delete that file of our brain like the ultimate computer programmer He is. I had never thought that through, but it makes sense. I hope and pray you're going to be there.

One of my very favorite Christian songs is "I Can Only Imagine" by Mercy Me. Every time I hear it, it makes me stop. It's a song about what you will do when you die and meet our Heavenly Father. It is truly beautiful and paints quite a picture of how you will respond to Him once you are in His presence. What will you do? What will I do? I don't know! I love all the options presented in the song, but I highly recommend this one from the Bible: "At the name of Jesus every knee should bow, in Heaven and on Earth and under the Earth, and every tongue acknowledge that Jesus Christ is Lord, to the glory of God the Father." (Philippians 2:10-11)

Please remember: You have so much ahead of you. Be purposeful and thoughtful in your decisions, but laugh every day, love deeply, and enjoy the beauty and experiences life has to offer. Life is truly a gift. Find your purpose, choose to be happy, use your gifts, love God, love others.

Let's end on a lighter note:

What is the best way to get to Paradise?

Turn right and go straight.

• • • Chapter 11 Questions • • •

1. What scares you about dying?

2. Whom do you hope to see in Heaven?

3. Have you completed the steps to get into Heaven?

If so, share your baptism experience.

If not, what is stopping you from making that commitment?

4. Your purpose—any thoughts?

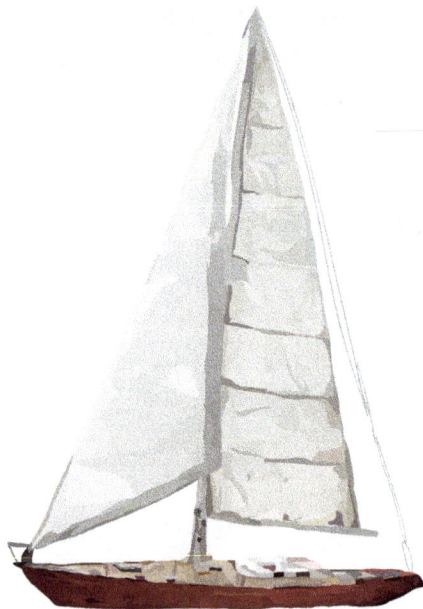

Jesus told her, "I am the resurrection
and the life. Anyone who believes in me
will live, even after dying."

John 11:25 nlt

CHAPTER 12

Money

A man asks, "God, how long is a million years?"
God answers, "To me, it's about a minute."
The man says, "God, how much is a million dollars?"
God answers, "To me, it's a penny."
The man says, "God, may I have a penny?"
God answers, "Wait a minute."

Money: No need to search for an attention grabber here! I would be remiss if I did not offer you some advice in this area as well. However, this is not my area of expertise. Luckily, I married someone with a great mind for numbers. I have teased my husband, Rusty, that English is his second language; numbers is his first. He's a talented CFO, brilliant CPA, accomplished negotiator, and all-round smart businessman. That picture you may have in your head of a CPA/CFO—throw it out the window. He is not your typical that. He has many gifts: leadership skills, generosity, athleticism—in thirty years, there's not one sport I've seen him do poorly. And he gets along with all kinds of people. He is a down-home country boy who can talk to bankers and lawyers with ease. Not to mention, our yard is the envy of all our neighbors as well. Rusty is unique.

Numbers is the area where he thrives. Words, not so much. In the Atlanta airport recently, he asked, "Do you know you can get a rectal scan for TSA pre-check?"

"Do you mean a *retinal* scan?" I asked. (I knew what he meant—that comes with being married for over thirty years.) In his mind, rectal, retinal—whatever. (Can you picture TSA giving rectal scans at the airport? Tee hee hee.) He always makes me laugh. As a CPA and CFO, he chose a profession where his gifts are put to good use. He takes care of many people, helps people every day, and loves it. I'm very proud of him. Further, I'm sure God is pleased that he is using his gifts to help others.

Naturally, I have relied on him for information in this chapter. He has been a wonderful provider for our family. I don't know why God chose to bless us with so much. As I mentioned earlier, I am now a retired schoolteacher. I always thought it was unfortunate that teaching required so much time, energy, and expertise, yet did not receive the monetary reward it deserves. Teachers are highly underpaid, and they have to do it all with very little. A salute to all teachers! You should choose a vocation that makes you happy, regardless of the pay. Money is not everything. I want you to make sound financial decisions regardless of your income.

Here's a general outline to begin making a budget with your funds. At the top of the page write your salary, then begin subtracting.

- social security tax
- federal tax
- state & local tax
- tithe 10%
- health insurance
- 401k
- birth control
- rent/house payment/including insurance
- college loans
- utilities/phone/streaming/cable/internet

- car payment
- car insurance
- transportation/gas
- food
- household/personal items
- incidentals/rainy day fund (stuff breaks)
- entertainment
- vacation
- Christmas fund (The average household spends $1,536/yr. - fortunly.com.)
- pets (A dog or cat is $1,500/yr. - Business Insider.)
- Child (It costs at least $1,100/month - CBS news report.)

There will be other items pop up in your day-to-day living. The remainder of your funds can be used to put into additional savings, shopping online, or cash in your pocket.

Here are some helpful hints provided by Rusty and myself:

- **Live within your means!** Always, always pay off your monthly credit card balance and bills. If you don't have the money for it, don't buy it. If this is the only thing you learn in this section, you will be ahead of millions of Americans. So many people struggle in this area. Many, many are in credit card debt. *Don't get there.* If you do not have the money to pay for an item, then do not buy it and do not charge it. (House, car, and education excluded.)
- If your company has a 401k match, try to put in enough to get the entire match. For example, if they will match up to 5 percent of your pay, then put in 5 percent of your pay. This should be in your budget. *It is super important!*
- If you're living on a budget, don't buy a brand-new car. (I can afford a new car, but I often purchase a used car.) Also, don't let the car dealership tell you what you can afford. You need to

know that *before* you go shopping. The same goes for a house. You need to know what you can afford. Car salesmen and realtors have a formula they use to tell you what you can afford based on your income. It's a general formula so they know where to start, but I'm telling you: You need to know your expenses before you buy a house or car. YOU tell THEM what you want to spend.

- Once you get behind on payments, it damages your credit score. Once that is damaged, it is very difficult to bring it back up. You may not think that is a big deal, but your credit score is a *very big deal*. Keep up on all of your payments. If you don't, that's doing life the hard way.
- Get a roommate to share expenses.
- Make sure you have insurance—health, home, and automobile. This is a must. You can't afford *not* to have it. All it takes is one accident, and you could lose everything.
- Did I mention that children are expensive? Be preventative! Put birth control toward the top of your budget. It is important for your financial, physical, and mental/emotional health to pre-vent children if you are not ready for them. Abstinence is best, or use protection, and use it correctly.
- Try to earn scholarships toward your education.
- Try to earn college credits for free while you're still in high school.
- Go to a community college the first year or two to save money.
- Do not eat out every day, or even every other day. Limit it to once a week, if you must. Pack a lunch and cook your own dinner. Don't buy fancy coffees or frou-frou drinks frequently. Even if you can afford these things, they are so unhealthy, as well as expensive. It is not good for you physically or financially. Do the math and look at how expensive it is to eat out. **Learn how to cook!**

Everything you have is like owning ten apples

You may be thinking that you could easily take the 10-percent tithe to fill in where needed. I want to explain to you how Christians think of tithing.

Think of everything you have being represented by ten apples. God gave you those apples. They are His. He can take or add to those apples anytime He wants. As a Christian, God wants you to give Him back one of the ten apples out of love, faithfulness, thankfulness, and trust toward Him, so it can be used to forward His message to everyone. He wants us to give Him one of the ten that are His anyway. It all goes back to that choice thing. God could take them, but He wants us to choose to be faithful. It's a sign of our love for Him.

Maybe you're reading this and are very poor. It may be a struggle to just get food on the table. The teacher in me wants to put another plug in here for taking advantage of a free education. You live in a country where you have a right to an education. You get to go to school! Every child gets to go to school! Maybe you don't like your school. I can't really help that, but I can tell you that the majority of teachers are hard-working, caring people. I know there may be some bad ones, but every profession has some bad ones. You need to take advantage of the education that is right in front of you. Please value education! If you don't want to be poor, education is your ticket out. Think of your schooling as a buffet, and it's all you can eat! All you have to do is go and consume whatever you want. Take advantage of it. It's free. Eat (learn) everything you can!

The elementary and junior high schools that I went to were the poorest schools in our city. Quite often there would be fights behind the dry cleaners near the school—boys or girls, blacks or whites—it didn't matter. I was always afraid I would get beat up, so I kept my mouth shut. Perhaps that's why I was so shy for many years. The teachers would always tell my mom at conferences that they couldn't even hear me when I read aloud in class. I kept my mouth shut but my eyes and ears open. I had great teachers and parents who valued education. I was able to succeed. You can too.

Everything that you learn is power. We tend to think of money as power, but having an education is also powerful. Having an education will benefit you in many ways, from your day-to-day living to your vocation. It will help you in any and all aspects of life.

Along with skills and experience, language and appearance help land jobs. When people meet you for the first time, your appearance makes a first impression before you even speak. (And yes, you only get one chance to make a first impression. So make it a good one.) Then, when you speak, people will form more opinions of you. I know we try not to judge others, but this comes unintentionally. People form opinions about your intelligence right away from how you talk. It's not fair, and it may not even be accurate. As a teacher, I admit I'm a bit of a grammar-police person. Sometimes after I say something, I think to myself, *Did I say that correctly?* I even police myself, so maybe it's just a curse of being a teacher. I also know I am definitely not always correct.

The English language is one of the most difficult languages to learn, or so I've heard. I believe it, because we Americans don't even know how to speak it correctly! Do yourself a favor and learn how to speak our language as well as you can. Learn how to conjugate a verb. Use the correct tenses. Learn how to spell and when to use *your* or *you're*; *there*, *their*, or *they're*; *was* or *were*; *saw* or *seen*. These are a few of the big ones people misuse every day. The way you speak and write can be so influential. Learn all you can in school about absolutely everything. All knowledge is power.

Since we're talking about your speech, there is something that is like nails on a chalkboard to me (you probably do not get that reference because no one knows what a chalkboard is anymore). Please do not get in the habit of saying, "Oh my God!" This was never allowed in our house. I realize it is accepted in our culture, but this becomes a bad habit. Use a thesaurus to find other ways to verbalize your astonishment. One of The

Ten Commandments is to not take the Lord's name in vain. This one gets abused *so* much. It is a commandment, so it is a big deal. Do not do it. "You must not misuse the name of the LORD your God. The LORD will not let you go unpunished if you misuse his name." (Exodus 20:7) ***God's name is to be revered.***

Money is power. Knowledge is power. Your words are also power. Think before you speak or type. Once it's out there, there's no taking it back. Even if you apologize, you've already caused some damage. Remember, God gave us two ears and only one mouth. Listen more than you speak. Use your words to build people up, for good works, and for praise.

I realize that you may not be at an age where you're thinking about some of the subjects I've mentioned, such as budgets. But I want to reemphasize that the choices you make now matter, and if you're not making them now, you will be soon. Everything you are learning now is important and will guide you in whatever direction you choose to go.

Your vices are like sprinkles on your sugar cookie

In life you'll be exposed to many things, and possibly you'll try some of them. Habits are formed very easily. Many bad habits are harmful and expensive. Do you remember how I said we all have a dash of talent on our sugar cookie? And how we all also have a pinch of vices? Off the top of my head, here are the vices I worry about getting a hold of you: addictions to drugs, alcohol, smoking or vaping, pornography, sex, phones, social media, gambling, shopping, and over- and under-eating, to name a few. We are all prone to weakness in some area. There is sin in this world, and the devil is rampant! Every single person is susceptible to any one of these offenses. No one is immune to temptation. No one.

I heard a sermon recently that said money and sex are all gifts from God, but they all come with responsibility. I know! I was shocked too! It was a little bit of a relief because I like those things. However, each of those are so easily abused by people, and *they are not to be abused*. It's a fine line that many people simply cannot walk.

You are old enough to be responsible for the decisions you will make about how you want to live your life. I'm trying to help you make decisions that will make your life easier. Now is the time for you to think about the kind of life you want to live.

Most people don't choose to be addicts; it happens slowly. You need to be aware and in control when you find something that you crave. I would hate for you to have a bad habit or addiction creep up on you. Be mindful if you think you're being tempted with something that could dominate your life.

Addictions are a struggle for people. It hurts not only the user but also the ones they love. Do not get caught up in any path that will lead you down a rough road. Life is hard enough without adding major hurdles that will not lead you to a successful, happy life. Think through what kind of life you want to have and how you can achieve those goals. Bad habits and addictions will not lead you where you most likely want to be.

No matter what, you will face some obstacles along the way. Addiction is a *huge* obstacle that many people simply never overcome. Some people work hard and eventually do overcome it, but it's a constant struggle for them to fight that addiction they worked so hard to defeat. Don't do life the hard way. Don't get started on something you'll come to wish you never had. Overcoming addictions is draining physically, emotionally, and financially on you and your loved ones. I don't want to neglect to mention the obvious, addictions could also cause you an early death.

Better yet, don't even choose those vices to begin with. Just don't! There are so many interesting sports, hobbies, crafts, music, etc. that you can delve into. Life is so, so good! Experience all you can to see what you really like or are talented in. Try new things. Put your energy into something positive. You can have fun without the vices. You will be blessed if you choose to live without the vices.

Vices are expensive

It's no coincidence that I waited to talk about vices in the money chapter. Addictions are expensive. They are a waste of good health, time, money, and energy. Use your health, time, money, and energy for good.

There are so many other faults that we are born with. I've only mentioned a few previously, but the world has many other evils we have to deal with, such as jealousy, greed, anger, hatred, revenge—and there are more. Plenty of evils await each of us daily. God gave everyone gifts, but unfortunately, everyone also has something that they struggle with. Not a soul on this earth is perfect.

My guess would be that it's hard to budget for an addiction or even for a vice. Do people include in their budget money for drugs? Alcohol? Sex? Or whatever it may be? I'd guess, no. Although, as adults, we could look at our expenses and see where the budget has been stretched or surpassed. That is an indicator of our weakness. At your age, you could look at your phone (adults can too). Our phones know very well what we like! What ads pop up for you? Matthew 6:21 is oh, so true, where you spend your money and your time is a good indicator of where your heart lies.

My Vices

Yes, I have faults. As I think about where to start on this topic, I realize this part is not near as much fun to write about. I'm not super talented, but I do have a couple of gifts God gave me that I discussed earlier, yet I have lots of things about me I would change if I had a magic wand. I guess it's only fair that I share some of those too.

I've lived long enough to see the rewards and ramifications of good and bad choices. Once I decided to live as a Christian the best way I could, I simply opted out of many of the evils of this world. This does not mean I am not tempted nor am I perfect.

My daily struggles with vices are not in the physical nature. Mine are more ethical. First of all, I try not to break the law every day. I tend to have a lead foot when I drive. I just really like to get where I'm going. I've gotten so much better, but it requires a conscious effort to obey the signs. That's also a reason I would never put one of those Christian fishes on the back of my car. I'm not a pokey driver, so I wouldn't want anyone to associate my driving habits with God. Also, I can be disappointed with my appearance. Glances in the mirror usually end with an eye roll or shrug of the shoulders. Oh, if I could have that magic wand for just one minute! I'd know exactly what to do! This, of course, leads to jealousy. Our society is always telling us how we should look. It's in our face constantly. My final vice that I deal with everyday, that I am not suppose to do, is worry. I worry about this world you are in. It is so messy and getting messier by the minute. You would be shocked if you knew how much I've prayed for you. We are not suppose to worry. The Bible says, "Therefore do not worry about tomorrow, for tomorrow will worry about itself. Each day has enough trouble of its own." (Matthew 6:34) I do trust God to take care of things; however, I want to be persistent so He knows exactly how important you are to me.

Financially, my vices have not been a problem for me. Other than the occasional speeding ticket, I've been fine. However, if I want to replace that magic wand with a surgeon, I'm going to have to do some figuring!

There you have it! Those are the daily struggles I have. Honestly, I do not spend much time dwelling on the law breaking, jealousy, or tiny bit of self-loathing. The worrying about stuff could use improvement. You can see I am not perfect nor am I exempt from vices or temptations. I could complain more about myself, but honestly, I've been so blessed. My life could be a whole lot worse. I prefer to enjoy what God has given me and all life has to offer and try not to let the vices and temptations of this world lead my life. Don't be misled; vices and temptations are always going to be there. It's a constant struggle to fight them. Some days we do better than others. The choices I have made in my life led to multiple blessings on me. Even though I am not outstanding in any one area, I choose to be happy with what God gave me. He loves me, for the bad in me and all. God loves average, ordinary me. God loves *me*! (And you too!)

My nature tends to run toward "the-glass-is-half-full" point of view. I can find positives in any situation. It's hard for me to be Pessimist Penny in this chapter, but this world has so much to worry about. I do believe that money and sex are wonderful gifts from God, but I see so many people abusing them. People will allow any one of these to be the driving force in their lives. Each of these can be an evil compulsion. My hope and prayer is that you would learn to enjoy life without these distractions. Be alert! Watch out for the vices and temptations that surround you everywhere you look (ads, music, friends, etc). *Learn self-discipline.* It's a must in our society, if you plan on being successful.

In conclusion, money is not everything. It certainly cannot buy happiness—that is true. But I'm not going to lie: Life is easier if you don't have to spend all your free time worrying about paying the bills. Also, marriage is hard enough, so if you can eliminate one more issue to stress about, that would be extremely beneficial. According to a Ramsey Solutions study, money arguments are the second leading cause of divorce, behind infidelity. It will be helpful to have a spouse that is on the same page as you with mutual (thoughtful) spending habits.

I hope and pray you're successful for many reasons, not just financial ones. Work should be rewarding and challenging for you. However, again, you'll enjoy life more if all your spare thoughts don't constantly drift toward making enough money to meet your needs. I want your spare thoughts to be on positive, Godly speculations.

If you are successful financially, that would be wonderful! Be generous. Share. Give to others. It always amazes me how easy it is to make someone's day. Buy someone's lunch in the drive-thru line. Add their items to yours at the dollar store. Drop off a ham for Christmas dinner.

You can be more generous with high-dollar amounts too. Do it cheerfully. If that's hard for you, practice. Once you experience others' joy, it makes your heart happy too.

Moderation and self-discipline are critical. That's the best financial advice I'll leave with you. Giving and sharing just makes you a wonderful, compassionate person. The Bible says, "People who long to be rich fall into temptation and are trapped by many foolish and harmful desires that plunge them into ruin and destruction." (1 Timothy 6:9) Money is not everything.

I have a coaster in my car that says:

Live simply

Speak kindly

Care deeply

Repeat

I love that car coaster. It's a daily visual reminder for me.

I'll end with a joke about money.

There was a wealthy man near death. He had worked very hard for his money, so he wanted to take it with him to Heaven. He prayed that this would be possible.

An angel informed him that God had decided to allow him to bring one suitcase with him. The man was thrilled! He found the largest suitcase he could and filled it with pure gold bars. He placed it beside his bed.

After he passed, he showed up at the Gates of Heaven, but St. Peter said, "Hold on, you can't bring that in here!"

The man explained that he had special permission. St. Peter verified his story and said he was supposed to check the contents before letting it through.

St. Peter opened the suitcase to see what precious worldly items the man brought. Then he said, "You brought pavement?"

"And the twelve gates were twelve pearls, each of the gates made of a single pearl, and the street of the city was pure gold, transparent as glass."

(Revelation 21:21)

Things money can't buy:
1. Manners
2. Morals
3. Respect
4. Character
5. Common Sense
6. Trust
7. Patience
8. Class
9. Integrity
10. Love

It cannot buy your eternity either.

• • • CHAPTER 12 QUESTIONS • • •

1. What tempts you?

2. Reflect on the budget. Do you see any problems with it? Are there any surprises? Where do you disagree?

3. Do you know someone with poor spending habits? Do you know a saver?

4. Do you think you could tithe?

5. Think about how much you eat out. Self reflect here.

6. Do you treasure your education?

7. Do you judge poor grammar? Do you have room for improvement?

8. What is power to you?

9. Do you have any vices/faults? Do you worry about vices? What are the pros and cons of these vices in your daily life?

10. Do you know an addict? If so, do you see ways that their addiction has impacted their daily life?

11. Do you think it's difficult to never partake of worldly vices and temptations?

Do not conform to the pattern of this world, but be transformed by the renewing of your mind. Then you will be able to test and approve what God's will is—His good, pleasing and perfect will.

ROMANS 12:2 NIV

CHAPTER 13

My Book Journey

I became a Christian when I was in the fourth grade. After school, sometimes I'd go to my friend Jana's house for a snack and a little Bible group. One day she came to my house, up the stairs in that little back bedroom where I did my homework (I am reminded here of the Miranda Lambert song "The House That Built Me"; sometimes I think in song lyrics). I got on my little knees, folded my little hands, and spoke to God like I was talking to a friend (Cue the Rodney Atkins song "Watching You"—I'll stop now), and she led me in a prayer asking God into my heart. I believe God's Holy Spirit entered me right there. That decision I made as a little girl impacted the rest of my life. This really causes me to pause. It's hard to believe that the little fourth-grader, whom I honestly do not remember, made a decision that not only impacted my entire life but also my eternity! Please understand that decisions you make now impact your life. I may not have realized the gravity of that decision at the time, but it most certainly did matter.

I proceeded along in life, going to church with my mom, living a normal life, not real "churchy." But I did make major decisions based on what I believed would meet God's approval and the definition of a "good girl." I assume that my school friends most likely saw me as a "good girl," not necessarily a Christian girl. They are not the same thing. I don't remember ever stepping out of my comfort zone to stand up for God as a child. While I may have been a good girl, I'm sure I didn't radiate Christianity.

People who have a love for Jesus in their heart are different. Especially when you know someone pretty well, then suddenly there's something different about them, but you can't identify it. Maybe I should only speak for myself. Looking back, I recognized the peculiarity of my mom becoming suddenly different.

Part of being a "good girl" was doing everything in the right order—graduate high school, go to college, get engaged, get a good job, get married, then lose my virginity and begin a family after a couple of years. Meanwhile, go to work, work hard, raise our family, and so on. I have no regrets doing these things in this order. It made my life easier, better, richer. I do believe God has blessed me for being faithful.

Side note: Again, I am not trying to give the impression that this made me the perfect little Christian girl. I definitely was not. There are people who can tell you I wasn't; I still am not and never will be. I could give you names, but I won't! I'm just trying to do the best I can. That's all anyone can do. When you mess up, you ask for forgiveness and try to do better next time. That's it. You're forgiven. That's called God's mercy. Isn't God's mercy wonderful?

I truly didn't become close to God until my sort-of-perfect life came to a halt when our son was born. We went through his three open-heart surgeries during my early thirties. I believe that many prayers got him through. I had to rely on God to get through it. It was one of those times when all I could pray was, "Help me, God." And sometimes you hurt too much to pray at all. But God knows your heart, and when you surround yourself with Christian people, they will pray for you when you can't. The Holy Spirit in me prayed for me when I couldn't. "In the same way, the Spirit helps us in our weakness. We do not know what we ought to pray for, but the Spirit himself intercedes for us through wordless groans." (Romans 8:26) I don't know how people get through rough times without Him. God gave me strength, comfort, and eventually peace.

After God helped us through that difficult time, I decided to be baptized again. I was baptized as an infant, but I wanted to do it again to show God that I had chosen to follow Him since there are no examples of infants being baptized in the Bible. I truly loved Him and wanted to walk closer with Him. I told God, "Thank you for all you've done for me and my son. To show my thanks in some small way, I promise to give thanks to you at every meal, no matter who I am with or where I am seated." I realize that's nothing compared to what He did for me, sacrificing His son for imperfect me. I not only wanted to thank Him for my blessings three times a day, but I wanted to show the world that I'm thankful for my blessings. I am proud to honor Him wherever I am, whoever I'm with.

I also used to randomly include in my prayers a long time ago to God, "Let me do something great for you. Use me to do something great for you." Of course, I tried to envision in my own small mind what that might look like as a teacher, wife, mother, church-goer. Honestly, I had no idea what He could do with me, but I threw it up there anyway, just in case He thought I could do some good somewhere.

I'm wondering if this idea for a book is my chance to do something for Him. If it helps someone think about His existence or what choices to make, it'll be worth it. My hope and prayer is to bring glory to God and win some souls (especially yours) for Jesus.

Then again, maybe this isn't it. All I know is, during the past year and a half, I had the idea to write you. There were fleeting thoughts, and then they became more prevalent. They also continued to persist with daily scriptures constantly reminding me that He is with me and outside influences that have become almost too many to keep track of, so much that I conceded to write to you. I argued with God for at least a year. Here are the events that led me to begin this endeavor.

How I came to write this book

First, about twenty years ago, I went to hear a speaker at church and bought the book *Answers in Genesis* by Ken Ham. It discussed many scientific facts about how the Bible is correct and that science is also proving it to be true. I was elated that finally more people may be led to worship God, because I so often hear, "I believe in science, not God." However, I did not understand why this wasn't the top story on the news. Evidently, the science world wasn't ready to embrace all the evidence the book had to offer. Either way, science and religion weren't in complete harmony just yet. I visited the Creation Museum, and it looked scientific to me. I was still very hopeful that the Bible and science would finally mesh, with no room for doubt. Every time I hear of a study or progress made in the medical world or science world, I think how amazing God is! The more scientific, the better. This world and our complex bodies, in my mind, cannot be made randomly from scratch. To me, science is nothing but proof that a higher being is the master designer. Random occurrences do not create masterpieces.

Second, in 2017 to 2018 my children were growing up, moving out, settling down, and yet, no grandchildren. Now that I'm retired and getting older, I did the math and realized I'm not going to be around very long to have an impact on the lives of my future grandchildren. I thought to write a book to share who I am, what I have learned, and why I believe what I believe. It has helped to relieve the sense of ambiguity about my grandchildren and my role in their lives. Grandchildren, I am now able to tell you everything I want. Then I can die with a clear conscience, knowing I have done my best to expose you to God's truth.

Our community has also had many young people dying by suicide in recent years. It makes my heart break for them and their families. Every time I hear of another loss of a young person, it makes me wish I could have talked to them and told them that life will get better. They're just in an extremely bad season that is a mere snippet of time in their glorious life. We all have them to some extent. But it will pass! You are loved! You have a purpose! My heart is troubled for their families. I'm hoping this book can reach other young people too.

In September 2018, events happened that forced me to think seriously about this project.

I attended a church service in Greensboro, Georgia, where the preacher on a video discussed how he has begun to change his verbiage in his sermons. He doesn't preach "as it is written in the Bible" any more, because many people simply don't accept that if it's in the Bible, it's true. Many from my generation grew up accepting the Bible because that's what we heard in church, and we just accepted it. But now church attendance is dwindling. Believing everything in the Bible just because it is written there does not make it fact to many people. The preacher explained that he now says, "as it is *recorded* in the Bible." He believes we need to focus on the *acts* recorded in the Bible and other places. We believe in Jesus because he came like he said he would, he died like he said he would, and he arose like he said he would. That's why we believe—because of these acts, not just because it is written down, but because these acts were written in several places, so we can know that they actually occurred.

I had thought that using the Bible to preach to you if you don't believe in God may not be the most effective way for me to convince you, and this was an affirmation that maybe that wasn't such a crazy idea. I just had never heard anyone else say that the Bible alone doesn't carry the same weight for unbelievers as it does for me, so using the Bible to introduce unbelievers to God may not be the most effective plan. This realization gave me confidence to share my beliefs through other channels.

In November 2018, my church small group practiced telling our stories of how we came to be Christians, so we'd be prepared when we were in a situation where we had a chance to witness to others. We each had two minutes. We practiced telling our story to the group, then shared it with someone outside of church. Soon after we were invited up for the weekend by friends in Green Bay to attend a Packers game (we didn't have to think long on that invitation). While I was at the airport in Chicago, I decided to pick a stranger to practice telling my story to. I thought, what the heck? I'll never see them again. I'm only asking for two minutes. It'd be good practice for me because it's something I'm definitely not comfortable doing. Let me try this and step out of that comfort zone.

Let me interrupt my story here and tell you that it was so difficult to find a person in the food court who didn't have their nose in their phone. If I attempted to approach anyway, they went deeper into their phone. Smiling and making eye contact alone was a difficult task.

I finally saw one person waiting to order his breakfast who looked approachable. He was actually watching me and said he knew I was on some mission. We chatted for a little while. My two-minute story did not go as practiced originally, but that's okay. That's why it's good to practice. To my surprise the man was an author, Gaylan D. Wright, author of *Slave to the Dream*. Since I had been thinking about writing a book, I thought, *That's funny, God, because I was thinking about writing a book, and you put an author in my path. I get it. Very funny.*

Then my dad passed away in December 2018 from pancreatic cancer. (He was such a good man with a great sense of humor. He was a hard worker, loved being at home and loved his family, loved fixing things, and loved a good joke or funny story. I miss him. My brother is a lot like him. They both are beloved by all who know and knew them.) Afterward, my mom went on a rampage cleaning out every nook and cranny in their house, throwing away or giving away anything she could. She had told dad she'd be coming right behind him and didn't want us kids to have the burden of going through a bunch of stuff. That's how she came to find Grandma's poem, which reminded me that my grandchildren won't know me like I didn't really know my grandma.

In April 2019 I went with my husband to a golf tournament in Georgia. We visit there often. For some reason, on the first night, the wives had a separate dinner from the men. The first person I met was a talented woman, Dorothy Andreas. She has many accomplishments, but low and behold, most recently she had written a book, *Streamline Success: Eliminate Chaos from your Service Business*. She sat at my table with me. This definitely got my attention. When she said she was an author, I stopped in my tracks. Chills went down my spine. Then I thought, *God, are you serious?* Maybe God thought that since I ignored the first author He put in my path, this time He'd put an author right in front of me for the evening, who could share her knowledge of writing a book. Maybe God thought, *You're going to ignore my sign? Let me make myself more clear!* After only knowing Dorothy about an hour, I stood behind her in the buffet line and told her I thought God wanted me to write a book. She shared her publisher's name, a book with tips on writing a book, and an autographed copy of her book. These were very helpful.

Conceding, I decided to take some notes to see if I really had enough to say, just to prove to God that I could not write a book. Nonetheless, I started taking lots of notes! At times I could not write fast enough.

In May 2019 we were on a vacation in Marco Island, Florida, and I went to a church there. I love to attend church services at different places. Before the service began, the church shared a quick video from the author of *Answers in Genesis*. This brought back all the feelings I had from years ago about using science and statistics to demonstrate the existence of God.

In June 2019 my mom's church had *one last ticket* for someone to join them in their van to visit the Ark Encounter, a replica of Noah's Ark in Williamstown, Kentucky. Imagine that! I felt like signs to write a book were coming at me from all directions now. The experience gave me the strong urge to share my thoughts on how this world we live in and the bodies we own could not have been formed accidentally; I especially wanted to share them with my wonderful family. At this point, though, I was still going back and forth: Was I being led to write a book or was it my imagination? To be honest with you, it was a lot harder than I anticipated, and I was hoping it was my imagination. I had pretty much decided I would write it, though, because at least it would give me a chance to tell my grandchildren about me and, more importantly, about God. But I had another trip planned—a big trip to Skye, Scotland, in July. I told God, "Okay, I'll write a book. I will finally start digging in, taking my notes and getting them organized. I will start the whole writing process…when I get back from Scotland." Amid all the ideas I was jotting down, I felt compelled to continue what I had started. I just kept saying, "When I get back from Scotland…" My plan was to wait until my traveling was done so I could really focus.

The entire time I was in Scotland, I kept looking around for more signs from God. It got to a point where I was looking over my shoulder every day waiting for another sign. It was that much on my mind. Even while I was hiking up and down mountains with my family, their friends, and sheep, I was waiting for more acknowledgement from God. But I didn't see any there.

The only signs I saw were His brilliant masterpieces of nature everywhere I looked, but there was nothing that told me to write a book. Whenever I travel and see the mountains, or the ocean, or hear thunder, it always reminds me of God's omnipotence. Quite frankly, it intimidates me. The part where God is to be feared: check. I believe He is powerful. I always remember right after that, though, that God is also love. The beauty of Scotland was a constant reminder of God's artistry, so I felt close to God there—but no signs.

However, the very day I returned from Scotland, my mother-in-law, Libby, passed away. She'd had a stroke three and a half years ago and was suffering a long, slow death. Hospice had been involved with her care in recent months. We were glad she was no longer suffering because it had gone on so long. She no longer ate or talked to us or even opened her eyes, because her eyelids hurt. We had been taking turns being by her side, so I had been driving to visit with her two or three times a week. Remember that I had put God on hold, saying, "When I get back from Scotland,

Lord, then I'll dive into writing." When Libby died on that exact day I returned, I felt as if God was saying to me, a known procrastinator, "Now you have no more excuses. Libby is home and is no longer suffering. Your schedule is completely clear." I felt as though He used that timing of the inevitable to clarify what He wanted me to do. God used a time of sadness to influence me to do something good. That is such a God thing for those who have the Holy Spirit. He will always use terrible situations and somehow bring goodness to light if you have Him participating in your life. That's because He loves us.

I dug in as soon as we put Libby to rest. I took my notes, started reading them, and they did not sound good! It was disappointing and overwhelming at times. I continued to get in my head and think, *What am I doing? I can't do this! I must be imagining things. Please, let me be imagining this!* The devil will tempt you and tell you you're not good enough.

This reminds me of the song "Nobody" by Casting Crowns:
So when I hear that devil start talking to me, saying,
"Who do you think you are?" I say,
I'm just nobody trying to tell everybody
All about Somebody who saved my soul.

The devil tells me that all the time. "What do you think you're doing?" I just keep singing the rest of the verse: I'm just nobody trying to tell everybody all about Somebody who saved my soul!

Then God sent me another message that again stopped me in my tracks. He was relentless. In July 2019 we had a small group meeting with my lady church friends. My friend Stephanie showed up with a Christmas present she had forgotten about and found stuck in a corner. And this was July. Out in the parking lot of the church, she gave it to me, and it was a beautiful journal. I was stunned. Speechless. Chills again. It was the final nudge I needed. It was blank pages, and I believe God was telling me to fill them. This was the last time I doubted what God wanted me to do. The timing of that gift was perfect. I have never questioned Him again.

Soon after that, Rusty and I attended a Michael Bublé concert in Columbus, Ohio. He and I rarely attend concerts together, but I told him I wanted to go, so he caved in. During the song "I Just Haven't Met You Yet," I knew that was the title of my book. It was so very plain to me. I just knew it.

I continued writing. I had something for every chapter except the chapter about death. I had been putting it off because, well, it's death. A friend of Libby's whom neither Rusty nor I knew sent us a sweet letter about Libby's passing in July. It included scriptures about death to comfort us. I felt it was another little prod (that I was constantly needing) telling me to continue writing. There was one chapter I had delayed starting, and I was provided with encouragement as well as content.

I had begun my introduction, writing about my memories on the farm, when my cousin, Cheryl, who was evidently reminiscing, asked my mom if she had any pictures of the farm. I volunteered to make copies for Cheryl, and it occurred to me again how coincidental events were happening as I was writing since I had just been rehashing those old memories myself.

I believe that when you are doing what God intends for you to do, he will continue to encourage you along the way.

In October, my days were spent muddling around with the first and second chapters of this book. I wasn't sure how to proceed on those topics. Several ideas were going around in my brain. One day when it was on my mind, Drew Brees came across my social media with a quote: "We live by faith, not by what we see." (2 Corinthians 5:7) Again, it caused me to stop in my tracks. It just jumped out at me. It was a Bible verse I'm sure I had heard before, but I don't remember when or where. It was exactly what I needed to hear at that moment. It's such a sweet, simple, powerful verse that I now think about often, a reminder that it really doesn't matter what the science says at any one point in time, because Christians know that God exists and will reveal Himself to us when He deems it necessary. God doesn't want us to have a blueprint. He wants us to believe first. For now, we simply need to live by faith.

I also want to reemphasize here that reading God's Word is another way that He speaks to you. When you ask God for guidance and verses jump out at you, that is Him speaking to your heart.

According to Rick Warren, there are four ways God will speak to you:

- through the Bible
- through teachers
- through impressions (an event or words that leave an impression on your heart that coincides with God's Word)
- through our circumstances

I have experienced all these things while writing to you. Thank you for that. This experience has made me feel closer to Him.

If you feel God is telling you to do something, listen and pray for guidance and read your Bible faithfully. He will provide you with encouragement. Be open to finding signs.

Ask God for guidance on everything. What college should you attend? What should you major in? Should you go to college? Should you marry that person? Should you take that job? Should you buy that house? (Also, remember, you should take *everything* to Him in prayer, not just the big stuff.) "Do not be anxious about anything, but in every situation, by prayer and petition, with thanksgiving, present your requests to God." (Philippians 4:6-7) Then you have to be patient and wait for His answer. Read the Bible. Look for signs—more than one sign. No sign may also be an answer—possibly "no." But be persistent. Listen to the Garth Brooks song "Unanswered Prayers." It has a great message to it. The moral of the song is that unanswered prayers can be a blessing. "Some of God's greatest gifts are unanswered prayers" is the main line. Sometimes God has bigger plans for you than what you're asking for. He can provide so much more than we can even imagine. You have to trust in God. If you don't pray about everything, you're rolling the dice and taking a chance. Let God tell you because He knows what's best for you. Let Him shed His grace on you. You gotta ask, though. If you're not praying and reading the Bible, you are just hoping to get lucky, hoping things will work out well for you. Maybe they will. Maybe they won't.

And don't be asking God to give you a sign to do anything that would be revengeful or cruel to others. If you think you see signs for that, that's the devil working on you. Remember, you are here to serve and love God and to serve and love others. He will never ask you to do anything that would be vindictive or hateful. If you have those feelings, please find someone trustworthy and ask for help. If that person wasn't able to meet your needs satisfactorily, ask another person. Don't give up on asking for help. That's not a crime or a sin. We all need help at some point.

After all of these events and my constant struggle with God, I continued feeling urged to do something that I may or may not be capable of doing; yet I always told myself He certainly wouldn't ask me to do something and then leave me stranded. I always knew that if He wanted me to do this, I must be able to do it. Then I was reminded of a joke from the movie *Pursuit of Happyness*. It goes something like this:

> A man was in the water starting to drown. A boat came along and the driver said, "I'll help you!"
>
> The drowning man said, "My God will save me."
>
> Another boat came along and this driver yelled, "We will help you aboard!"
>
> But the drowning man replied, "My God will save me."
>
> The third boat found the man struggling and the driver said, "We can help you!"
>
> The drowning man responded, "My God will save me."
>
> The man eventually drowned. When he got to Heaven, he asked, "God, why didn't you save me?"
>
> God's response was, "I sent you three boats!"

That man did not know how to read God's signs! When I die and stand before God, I don't want to say, "God, I didn't write this book because I wasn't really sure if I was meant to," or "God, I thought I was imagining those signs," or "God, it wasn't really clear to me," or "God, you could've talked to me with a burning bush." I don't want to hear Him say, "I sent you two authors, two videos, a clear schedule, and a blank note-book! Yes, I wanted you to write a book!" I want to hear Him say instead, "Well done, my good and faithful servant." (Matthew 25:21) So this is me being a faithful servant to God.

I know some nonbelievers have complained that if Christians really believed all that Bible stuff, they should be running around trying to save everyone. How could they let their loved ones burn in Hell? How could you be so unassertive?

The problem is, when you hear people yell it on the street corners, people roll their eyes. We generally just try to be kind to our fellow humans and hope they can see our love for Jesus in our acts of kindness. We want to beg you to convert, but people don't like religious fruitcakes. You can't come on too strong—it turns people off. Actually, I agree with that complaint; it's just too important to me that my grandchildren, and everyone, should come to know and follow Jesus. Therefore, I will not be silent. This is my attempt to shout on a street corner. I can live the rest of my life peacefully knowing that I have tried to share this good news with anyone who would listen. This information is way too important to not share with you, even though I just haven't met you yet.

• • • Chapter 13 Questions • • •

1. Have you ever felt led by God to do something?
2. How did you become a Christian?
3. Do you ever think in song lyrics?
4. How do you think others perceive you?
5. Have you ever hurt so badly you couldn't pray?
6. Have you ever stepped out of your comfort zone for Jesus?
7. How has God spoken to you?
8. When are you reminded of God's power?
9. Have you ever felt not good enough?
10. Have you ever had a Bible verse jump out at you?

May the Lord give you understanding in all things.

2 Timothy 2:6 NKJV

CHAPTER 14

Miscellaneous

The majority of what I wanted to say to you has been said. However, there are some miscellaneous items I couldn't fit in anywhere else, so this is my miscellaneous chapter with random things I want to share with you in no particular order.

SPORTS

I wish I had been able to reference sports more in this book. I didn't play sports, so I have no experience to relate, but I think sports are valuable. You learn many life lessons when you play. It's something you can enjoy the rest of your life, if not as a player then as a spectator. Even though I didn't talk about sports much in this book, I want you to know that I respectfully admire them, enjoy them, and highly recommend your participation in them.

I was part of the drill team in high school for three years. I learned a lot about self-discipline (a tremendous trait to learn that has benefited me throughout my life), endurance, responsibility, teamwork, and competition—all worthy traits that are learned in sports. (Thank you, Mr. Carpenter.)

I also have a special place in my heart for football. When people talk about comfort food, nothing particular comes to mind for me. But football is comforting to me. It was always on while I was growing up. It reminds me of home. There's nothing like a bunch of grown men tackling each other to soothe the soul with that homey feeling!

BEAUTY TIPS

I'm no beauty queen, but these are things I recommend for granddaughters and grandsons (mostly):

- Bathe daily, especially at your age.
- Always remove your makeup when you go to bed.
- Always moisturize in the morning and evening.
- Put on perfume/cologne before your jewelry.
- Pat yourself dry after bathing—don't rub your skin.
- Drink eight 8-ounce glasses of water a day. It's recommended for hydration, and it does wonders for your skin.
- When applying makeup, accent your eyes OR your lips, not both; it's too much if you do both.
- Smile! It makes you more beautiful!
- Learn what colors look best on you. Pay attention when people compliment your clothing.
- Exercise regularly and eat healthy. This is for your physical appearance and your physical well-being. It will make you feel better mentally as well.
- Brush your teeth at least twice per day and floss daily. Oral hygiene is a must.
- Have good posture: Sit up straight, shoulders back, head high. Be proud of who you are. My mom was always telling me to put my shoulders back.
- Only buy zero to three trendy pieces per season—the rest should be classics.
- Be careful with shopping. Buying stuff all the time is a mindset.

Trends change because retailers need you to continue spending your money. It helps the economy. They make it; you buy it. They improve it or change the style so you want the newer version. It's what makes this world go round. The almighty dollar is the driving force of just about everything.

I want you to control your wants. Fortunately, I do not have strong urges to have the newest phone, a fancy car, diamonds, or extravagant vacations. I like all those nice things, and I do have nice things, but it's not what I need to be happy. Shiny things are impressive, but I don't want them to represent who I am. I choose not to become part of the superficial world of what I "gotta have" to be happy or accepted socially. Believe me, I can go shopping and put a dent in our credit card as easily as the next person. I'm not immune to wanting new stuff. I do have nice things, they just aren't the latest, biggest, or best version. Once you get in that mindset of having to have the best, there is most likely an underlying issue. Self-reflection is needed.

Do I actually follow all these beauty tips? Most, with the exception of exercising regularly. I am trying to drink lots of water, but I'm not sure how much exactly. Exercising—ugh. I feel so much better when I do it, it's just not fun for me. Sorry if you got those genes from me. I do believe it is essential. Physical work makes our bodies run more smoothly. You gotta do it.

Are tattoos okay? I don't know. I have not seen anything that I loved looking at more than a human body such that I want it permanently inked on me. I think they are trendy, and someday you may become regretful. However, if I lost a child or grandchild I may want something as a remembrance. Never say never. Personally, I can't see myself ever getting one, but I do not judge others who do it. *That's not my job*. It's personal preference.

Although, I do remember reading in a magazine once about a woman who tattooed a stemmed rose on the back of her neck, and as she aged it looked like a penis. Be forward-thinking in your tattoo choice.

On second thought, I found this Bible verse: "You shall not make any cuts on your body for the dead or tattoo yourselves: I am the LORD."

(Leviticus 19:28) I will definitely not be getting any tattoos.

Is plastic surgery okay? I don't know. I would have a lot of questions for you about why you want to do it. It's personal preference again. Part of me thinks that God made me this way for a reason. The argument goes, He also gave us intelligence to change. I suppose some people are so unhappy that they need it. I do not judge those who do it. *That's not my job.* Again, try not to get too caught up in your physical appearance. Your heart is what's important.

If you're already great-looking, good for you. *Don't let that be the only thing you're known for.* Plastic surgery? Pray about it and seek Christian counseling. It's important to know why you want it.

Do I have regrets? Yes.

I wish I had embraced Christianity earlier in life. When I think of what God has done for me, I can't help but wonder how different my life may have been if I'd known Him better sooner.

Also, recently something came across my social media that said, "Be careful what you tolerate; you're teaching people how to treat you." Boy, I wish I had seen that about forty years ago! As a person with a gift of patience, I tolerated more than I should have in some relationships. My expectations were too low. Set your bar higher.

I can think of several instances where I would love to have a do-over. There are definitely things I am not proud of. Overall, though, I wouldn't change much in my life. It's been pretty awesome. I'm very happy.

Do I ever doubt God's existence? Yes.

I hope and pray that's normal. I'm guessing this happens because I know people who do not believe, and I worry about their souls. I try to under-stand their point of view. They are fleeting thoughts, but I always go back to Jesus and the numbers: a man who was born, died, and resurrected, all as he predicted? His chance of fulfilling the prophecy was 1 in 100 quadrillion. There is a 1 in 700 quintillion chance of Earth being formed accidentally. Our perfect human bodies formed all by themselves? The process of birth?

No way all that is chance. In fact, looking at these numbers (even independently), doubting is not the smarter choice. Everything is too sophisticated to be random, and the way the pieces all fit together is pure perfection.

Further, when I think of all that God has done for me in my life, I could never turn from that. Looking at numbers and science doesn't take into account the feelings and love one experiences from walking with God. The closer you walk with Him, the more convinced you become of His love and righteousness.

When I have doubts, I just tell the devil to go away. I take control of my mind and thoughts. Then I make a choice, and I choose Jesus—all day, every day, every time.

Driving

Lord, why did you give me enough patience to work with disabled children for thirty years and enough patience to be married to Rusty for over thirty years, yet when I get behind Miss Oblivious going slow in the left lane on the highway, my patience goes out the window? Why, Lord?

This really has no significant life lesson, it simply allows me to have a chance to rant about a pet peeve of mine: people who drive in the left lane! The left lane is designed to pass slower cars in the right lane. This aids with traffic flow. If you are not passing anyone, you need to be in the right lane. Drive in the right lane—both literally and figuratively. When you don't, it makes me think you are inconsiderate, selfish, or just ignorant of traffic laws. How Christian do I sound right now?

I love to drive! I love to parallel park! Freaky, I know! There have been several occasions in my past where I have had speeding tickets, rightfully so. But I'm always aware of my surroundings. (Darn, there's that devil again.) However, I've gotten older and wiser. I'm not in such a hurry anymore, although I will never be a pokey driver—not aggressive, just not pokey. My lead foot is not as heavy as it used to be.

Speeding is stupid. Don't do it. Each of our children were told that a license to drive is a license to kill. Taking someone else's life would be…I can't even imagine what that would be like. I'm guessing it's something that would be with you for the rest of your life.

My husband used to like to tell me that speeding is a sin. I told him to show me that in the Bible. Actually, there are verses that talk about obeying the law of the land, for example, "Let everyone be subject to the governing authorities, for there is no authority except that which God has established. The authorities that exist have been established by God. Consequently, whoever rebels against the authority is rebelling against what God has instituted, and those who do so will bring judgment on themselves." (Romans 13:1-2) Here's another good one: "Obey your leaders and submit to their authority. They keep watch over you as men who must give an account. Obey them so that their work will be a joy, not a burden, for that would be of no advantage to you." (Hebrews 13:17) (Be respectful to policemen and policewomen. What a job they have! It is becoming increasingly difficult. Thanks to them all.) One more: "Keep God's laws and you will live longer." (Proverbs 19:16) I love those verses that are simple and right to the point. So don't be a criminal. Life will be much easier and pleasant if you're not. That's doing life the hardest way possible. Please do not lead a life of crime.

I almost forgot—don't mess with your phone while driving. Drivers under thirty years old are most likely to be using a cell phone at the time of a fatal crash (thesimpledollar.com). Especially if you are not right with God, you don't want to meet your Maker before you've made that choice and fulfilled your purpose. Yes, I know, there are lots of old people on their phones behind the wheel also. They need to stop it too.

HOLIDAYS

I believe that holidays are what YOU make of them. Halloween at our house was about dressing up in silly costumes, collecting and passing out candy, and some simple spooky decorations. That's it.

Do I think it's an evil holiday? I believe it can be if you want it to be. Yes, I believe in angels, and I also believe in Satan and his evil spirits. The Bible warns us to stay away from them, so they do exist.

"Demons are able to take shape, form, and be visible to humans."

Job 4:15

Core 52 explains that demons gain access most commonly through the occult (magic, astrology, etc.), sex, drugs, and dark music. They hate scripture being read or quoted aloud, praise (music), and praying aloud in Jesus's name.

Christmas for us is about celebrating Jesus's birth. We celebrate by giving gifts, and Santa did deliver them when the children were young. It is very easy for the secular world to embrace this holiday of giving. I never worry about this holiday going away. It does too much for business and the economy. Of course, it saddens me that more emphasis is put on Happy Holidays versus Merry Christmas to take Christ out of the holiday. Again, the holiday will become what you make of it. I say, "Merry Christmas!"

HUMILITY

This one should probably be an entire chapter. I see where there's at least seventy-three Bible verses on this topic. *God wants us to be humble.* Admit that you have imperfections and then try to correct them, knowing that you will never be perfect. Give God credit for everything, including those times you do really well. It's wonderful if you are great in some area(s)! I want you to be successful and proud but not to the extent of having to hurt others in the process or to show how great you have become. Be the best that you can be, but do not brag about it. In general, people do not like braggarts either.

"Humble yourselves in the presence of the Lord, and He will exalt you."

James 4:10

"Clothe yourself with humility."

1 Peter 5:5

I recently heard a speech by the great coach Lou Holtz. He advised graduates NOT to enter a room with the attitude, *Here I am!* Instead think, *There you are. How can I help?* (I also loved the part where he said, "It's never the right time to do the wrong thing, and it's never the wrong time to do the right thing.")

Pride is the downfall of many! "The LORD Almighty has a day in store for all the proud and lofty, for all that is exalted (and they will be humbled)." (Isaiah 2:12)

If you praise yourself, you will be humbled. If you are humble, you will be exalted. I think it's okay to be proud of yourself, but *always* give God the credit. Remember that God gave you your gifts to help others, not to make you look good.

Brushes with fame

Rusty did a professional athlete's taxes for a while. He also has played golf with Brian McBride, a former professional soccer player, and he had a couple business meetings with football great Joe Namath. He grew up in the same small town as Ray Miller, a baseball pitching coach who is a friend of the family.

In the early 1990s, we were at Pier 39 in San Francisco. I told Rusty that Joe Montana had just walked by. He didn't think I knew who that was. When he saw him then in the distance, he took off yelling, "Joe! Joe!" Joe didn't appear to hear him and proceeded to climb aboard a yacht. LOL.

In 2008 we had breakfast for the annual White House Easter Egg Roll with President Bush, The Jonas Brothers, Troy Aikman, Kyle Massey, and his brother, Christopher Massey. One of our girls helped Troy with his camera, and she had no idea who he was at the time.

I accidentally hit the back of Kevin Costner's chair with my beach bag at a private cafe on a beach in Florida. I apologized, but he didn't turn around. The two older women across from him just smiled at me, which at the time I thought was weird. I didn't realize who it was until a little later. We left him alone, except when Rusty decided to go chat with him while he was fishing from the shore.

We have a golf membership at the same place as Ben Roethlisberger, so we see him occasionally. One of these days I'll get the nerve to speak.

The celebrity I'd most like to meet is the Rock! *Oh, Dwayne!* That smile! I love a man who can laugh and has a kind heart. He appears to appreciate what he has and uses his fame to do good for others, as many celebrities do. Dwayne Johnson supports many charities, is very generous, and performs good deeds for his fans. Honestly, I'm not the star-struck type but possibly would be for the Rock.

I need to remind myself and you that celebrities have teams of people who work to sell us an image. Of course, we hope that these people are what we think they are, but we have no way to really be sure unless we're part of their inner circle.

It's fine to admire celebrities/athletes/musicians, but I suggest that you keep that in check. No celebrity is worthy of extensive amounts of your time and attention. Make sure you're spending more time and attention on God than on worldly things.

One of The Ten Commandments is that we are not to worship other gods. In our day and age, that means putting something else above God, such as worldly things like I mentioned above. God is a jealous God. "For the Lord your God is a consuming fire, a jealous God." (Deuteronomy 4:24)

The celebrity I'd like to play me when they *never* do a story about my life is Helen Hunt. I had a friend years ago who would comment occasionally that I reminded her of Helen. (I'm sorry, Helen Hunt.)

What have I found to be the best way to lose weight?

Eat less, exercise more.

That is the best way to lose weight. It's very simple. Putting it into practice is the hard part.

A Simple Philosophy

One of our girls had a poster on her wall in college that always stuck with me. It's a quote from Thomas Huxley, a philosophy you may want to consider embracing throughout your educational career and life: "Learn something about everything and everything about something."

Being Thankful

When you borrow or rent something, return it and leave it in better shape than you found it. Also, I hope your generation does not lose the art of writing a thank you note, even in an email if you must. Handwritten notes are preferable. People appreciate them if nothing else so they know that you received their gift. Manners are a beautiful thing.

Reading

Typically, if you're not very good at something, you avoid it. You choose not to participate. If reading is the thing that is most difficult for you, you don't get that option. My heart always hurt for those who struggled with reading. It's a problem that surrounds them every day. It can never be avoided completely. I spent the majority of my career working with children who had difficulty reading. I've mentioned teaching several times throughout this book, but I've yet to tell you what a great experience it was. I enjoyed working with children and other teachers. It was hard work, but I laughed every day. My hope is that when I die, God will show me how I was able to have an influence in the lives of these children. I hope and pray I had an impact on children with even more than teaching them learning objectives.

People Dissapoint

I don't care who comes to mind for you. I would disappoint you someday. I have disappointed people. People are not perfect. God is the only one you can depend on to be faithful and consistent. He will never disappoint you.

Of course, the world is full of admirable people. I have so many wonderful friends and family. I am blessed. I just wanted to remind you that we're all human. No one is perfect, and it's only a matter of time before you will realize that. Embrace those you love, even those you don't love, with all their imperfections. Be forgiving and ask for forgiveness when you need to. Remember, if you don't forgive others, God will not forgive you.

Why Christianity?

Maybe you're thinking, does it have to be Christianity? As long as you believe in something, isn't that the important thing? I have spent a lot of time explaining how and why I believe God is important. It matters, not only to me but also for your eternity, that you choose Christianity.

I admit, when I think about how all over this world people are born into their religion, it freaks me out a little that I could've been born a Buddhist, for example, if I was born in Japan. That is why it is so important to support missionary work all over the world. We want everyone to be exposed to God's truth. I am so thankful I was born in a country founded on religious freedom. I believe God has blessed our country because of that. As we veer further away from God in this country, I doubt that He is as pleased as He was initially. As we continue to lose our focus on Him, we go wildly astray. We will not receive His blessings if we continue to drift further and further away from Him.

I can't question why we were blessed to be born here where we have religious freedom. Again, I do not understand His ways, so I will simply say thank you for that enormous blessing. I cannot tackle the various religions of the world and how they came to be. All I can do is explain to you why Christianity is the best choice. Luckily, another weekly lesson from *Core 52* will explain why Christianity is different from all the others.

Mr. Moore explains that Christianity is different because of the incarnation, which means that God became man. There are three beliefs involved here that sets Christianity apart from any other religion.

> 1. **God is near.** God engages in our lives. He came to us
> through Jesus Christ. God is our Father, and we can have
> personal access to Him by knowing Jesus.
> 2. **God is love.** Other religions teach of love, but Christianity
> also teaches to love your enemies. Jesus's words on the cross
> reflect this: "Father, forgive them, for they know not what
> they do." (Luke 23:34) Jesus was the perfect example of how
> to love others.
> 3. **God suffered.** This idea is also unique from other religions.
> Jesus suffered on the cross for the sins of the world. Choose
> Christianity! It is real. It is truth. It is important for your soul.

Baptism

You know now how I love jokes. I'd like to leave you with one more here at the end. At least when I write jokes I don't screw up the punch line. Here's one my husband told me:

> The town drunk stumbled into church on revival Sunday. The
> preacher took him down to the lake, dunked him, and said,

"Have you found Jesus?!"

The town drunk said, "No!"

So the preacher dunked him again, leaving him under a little longer, and asked, "Have you found Jesus?"

Again, the town drunk sputtered, "No!"

So this last time, the preacher dunked the town drunk, leaving him under even longer, and asked, "Have you found Jesus yet?"

The town drunk stammered, "No, are you sure this is where he fell in?"

This joke reminds me of some people who get baptized and right away have overwhelming feelings of love for Jesus. It brings tears to my eyes when I witness their joy! I just want you to know that it happens differently for every person. Since I was a child when I first asked God into my heart, honestly, it was most likely out of fear. Then it grew to respect, and eventually love. That slow process was my fault. I was keeping God at arm's length. He was always right there ready to be more active in my life. It can happen very quickly if you're open to embracing all God has to offer.

My advice to you is to choose Jesus now, like right now, and then let your story unfold. Your story will be your story. As long as it's your desire to get to know Him, then choose Him right away, that's what's important. I wish I'd put forth the effort to know Him better so much sooner. I still want to learn so much.

SINNER'S PRAYER

Here is an example of a sinner's prayer you may use. Once you say it and believe it in your heart, you will become saved and born again. This is taken from preachwithgod.net.

Dear God,

I know I'm a sinner, and I ask for your forgiveness. I believe Jesus Christ is Your Son. I believe that He died for my sin and that You raised Him to life. I want to trust Him as my Savior and follow Him as Lord, from this day forward. Guide my life and help me to do your will. I pray this in the name of Jesus.

Amen.

• • • Chapter 14 Questions• • •

1. What sports, hobbies, and activities do you enjoy?

2. What beauty tips do you have?

3. Do you struggle with shopping and wanting stuff?

4. Do you ever doubt God's existence?

If so, what do you do?

5. Do you pray in school?

6. Are you humble? Give an example of how you could be more humble or less humble.

7. What famous person do you admire? Why?

8. What famous person do you most look like? Who would play you in your life story?

9. Is exercise part of your lifestyle?

10. Has anyone ever disappointed you yet?

11. Would you like to pray the sinner's prayer?

Therefore, as God's chosen people, holy and dearly loved,
clothe yourselves with compassion, kindness, humility,
gentleness and patience.

Colossians 3:12

CHAPTER 15

Conclusion

For someone who is described as quiet, I sure did have a lot to say! I feel better now. I can rest in peace. At least now you know who I am, or was, whichever the case may be. My intention was to not come across too preachy, but I'm pretty sure I did. Inevitably, that is who I am and what my experience has been. As much as I tried to reel in some of that evangelic soapbox instruction, in this conclusion, I'm going to *really* go "Holy Roller" on you. No sense holding back now! This goes back to my Lutheran roots. Here's what I believe:

THE APOSTLE'S CREED

> I believe in God, the Father Almighty,
> creator of Heaven and Earth.
> I believe in Jesus Christ, His only Son, our Lord.
> He was conceived by the power of the Holy Spirit
> and born of the virgin Mary.
> He suffered under Pontius Pilate,
> was crucified, died, and was buried.
> He descended into Hell.
> On the third day he rose again.

He ascended into Heaven
and is seated at the right hand of the Father.
He will come again to judge the living and the dead.
I believe in the Holy Spirit,
the holy Catholic Church,
the communion of saints,
the forgiveness of sins,
the resurrection of the body,
and life everlasting.
Amen.

During this time I've been writing to you, I've had moments where I've had tears in my eyes. I think it's the satisfaction of being able to express my love for you, give you some guidance, and know I've done what I felt I was led to do. I think God is pleased. At times I felt His presence. I could not have done it without Him.

I'm not sure if we'll ever meet or if I'll be of sound mind when we do meet. I've decided that if I do not meet you at all, it's okay. It is God's will. I accept that He knows it's best.

If my mind is gone when I finally meet you, I'm sorry. My fear is that I'll be one of those little old ladies who cuss like a sailor after a lifetime of never swearing. Please know that is not me. If I'm in a home when you visit, before you leave me, would you put on some music for me? When I would visit my sweet Libby in one of the homes she was in, I'd pass by this one room, and there was a little lady with her headphones on, eyes closed, both hands slightly raised at her sides, a big smile on her face, swaying back and forth. I hope that's me if my mind is gone. I want to be like her. I'll be in my own little happy place with music.

You get yourself to Heaven, and we'll have a lot to talk and laugh about. I hope and pray you make the right choice. I'll keep praying for you. Even though I haven't met you yet, you've had such an impact on my life. Thank you for providing me with the opportunity to please God and spread His Word.

Meanwhile, I have to figure out what to do next. One thing about retiring young—I don't feel ready to quit. Part of me wonders if I'm just beginning to fulfill my purpose. I'm going to continue practicing what I've been preaching and constantly shift my thoughts to God and wait to see where He leads me. I have a couple ideas to continue writing, or maybe He'll have something else in mind for me. Maybe I could share this book with other kids your age and help them through a difficult time. I hope you won't mind. Until then, I will be praying and anxiously awaiting to see what He has in store for me.

As I approach the end of this book, I find myself arguing with God again. I have been telling him, "Okay, God, here's my book. Our book. I'm not sure what to do next. Do we really have to publish it? I'm not sure I want to say, 'Hey, world, this is what I believe! Hey, world, these are my imperfections and character flaws! Hey, world, here's some struggles I've had!' Can't I just stay in my comfy little corner of the world with my wonderful family and friends? Is this really going to help anyone?" I wonder if God is tired of me dragging my feet, resisting, having little faith. I'm just a big old chicken. I'm scared of what the world will think. I'm even more scared of God not blessing me because I have not fulfilled my purpose. That terrifies me! However, I do have that choice. It would be very easy to play it safe. I guess I will proceed with the next steps. I recently heard that faith is like a muscle. You have to exercise it to make it stronger. I am going to choose faith.

This process of proceeding with the next steps took me several months. I procrastinated (again). I researched different publishing companies, and there was always something I didn't like. Then, "coincidentally," (again) I ran into my cousin Brenda, who mentioned that her granddaughter (Clair) had just graduated in graphic design and was working at a publishing company in the next town. Once again, God led me right where I needed to go. He knows me so well. I need Him so much.

As I reflect on this advice and experiences I've shared with you, I see that my life has been very blessed. I know that not everyone's life will be the same, but do you know the single best way that living a Christian lifestyle has been a blessing to me? I look at my children and son-in-law. All are wonderful adults. They are kind, thoughtful, fun, respectful, hard-working, and just wonderful people I am proud to call mine (and Rusty's). Living by God's principles has worked for Rusty and me. Thank you, Lord.

I'm going to leave you with scripture that my momma always tells me. I will hold God to this promise also, like she says she has claimed for her family.

Isaiah 44:3 says, "I will pour out My Spirit on your descendants, and my blessing shall be on your offspring."

I love you! God loves you more!

• • • Conclusion Questions • • •

1. Share something about one of your grandparents.
2. What do you believe?
3. Name something you have done that will be pleasing to God.
4. Can you let God guide you in all areas of your life?

For God so loved the world, that He gave his one and only son, that whoever belives in Him shall not perish but have eternal life.

John 3:16 NIV

Acknowledgments

At the top of my list, I must thank God Himself. This book would have never come to fruition if I did not feel His love and strength. All things *are* possible with God.

My husband, Rusty, has been a wonderful life partner in every way. He takes care of me and is my source of security, yet he challenges me to get out of my comfort zone and accomplish whatever I want to do. I thank him for allowing me to follow this dream. He never doubted me.

To my children, you are my pride and joy and my inspiration. Thank you for your commitment to our family and for the love you have for each other.

This process has taken me a while. Peggy was always checking up on me asking, "Where are we with the book?" She constantly encouraged me. Thanks, Mom.

Over the years, there have been many Sunday morning sermons that spoke to my heart. These preachers have a way of teaching God's Word. They have the gift of making you want to be a better person Monday through Saturday. Thank you for your teachings: Bill Meaige, Andy Stanley, and Mark Combs.

Last, but not least, thank you Emily, Clair, and Heather for helping me through this process. I treasure your gifts. It has been a joy to see what can be created when people work together using their God-given talents. I am blessed to be the recipient. Thanks for helping me navigate through this adventure. I could not have done it without you.

About the Author

Penny Deaton had a long, successful teaching career, a long Christian walk of faith, and a great family she loves to hang out with whenever she can. Her patience, easy-going demeanor, and honest personality have served her to teach and love on children of all ages and for serving the Lord in many capacities. She was born, raised, and continues to live in Zanesville, Ohio, but for fun, she can be found traveling south, on a boat on a lake, or having dinner with a friend. Her blessed, yet sometimes bumpy life experiences have given credit to writing her first book, *I Just Haven't Met You Yet.*

www.ingramcontent.com/pod-product-compliance
Lightning Source LLC
Chambersburg PA
CBHW051424090426
42737CB00014B/2817